A More Exciting Life

Published in 2020 by The School of Life

First published in the USA in 2021

930 High Road, London, N12 9RT

Copyright © The School of Life 2020

Designed and typeset by Dan Cottrell Studio

Printed in Latvia by Livonia

A proportion of this book has appeared online at www.theschooloflife.com/thebookoflife

Every effort has been made to contact the copyright holders of the material reproduced in this book. If any have been inadvertently overlooked, the publisher will be pleased to make restitution at the earliest opportunity.

The School of Life is a resource for helping us understand ourselves, for improving our relationships, our careers and our social lives – as well as for helping us find calm and get more out of our leisure hours. We do this through creating films, workshops, books, apps and gifts.

www.theschooloflife.com

ISBN 978-1-912891-25-2

10 9 8 7 6 5 4 3 2

A More Exciting Life

A guide to greater freedom,
spontaneity and enjoyment

The School of Life

Introduction

Some of what may be subtly yet importantly wrong with our lives can be traced back to the lack of a quality that could sound a little naïve or even unserious, but that is critically important to our flourishing: excitement.

When we lack excitement, it isn't that things are terrible: we may have work, friends, family and some options. It is just that, in a multitude of areas, life lacks flavour. Things feel repetitive, routine and devoid of intensity, as though we are merely going through the motions; as though we are there but are not properly present. Not much profoundly satisfies us; we fulfil obligations, we are dutiful and responsible, yet our deep selves are unquenched. Without meaning anything melodramatic by this, we are in a sort of cage. Or, to use another metaphor, we're crouching; our limbs aren't free. We are drained by varieties of shyness, numbness and inhibition.

Typically, we are invited to address the absence of excitement with outward manoeuvres: we are encouraged to travel, parachute out of aeroplanes or learn a foreign language. This is a book of psychology, however, and it holds that a lack of a sense of excitement primarily comes down to aspects of our minds – in particular, to difficulties we have first identifying and then feeling legitimate around our own desires and aspirations. Somewhere along the path of our development, we resigned ourselves too early to things that deserve to be protested against; we have felt too constricted (and perhaps unloved and unloveable) to communicate our truth to others; the proper expansion of our characters has been sacrificed for the sake of a now-stifling compliance.

This is a guide to recovering some of our spirit, and to becoming the sort of people who, thanks to a range of psychological reorientations, are connected to the intensity, beauty and mystery of life and to the richness of their own possibilities. The English psychoanalyst Donald Winnicott (1896–1971) once remarked that what mattered less than whether someone was happy or not was whether they felt as if they were leading *their own lives*. This suggests how often we fall into leading the lives that other people (some of them well-meaning) want us to lead, adjusting ourselves to their needs more than is wise and bowing to socially sanctioned but incomplete ideas of what is 'normal'.

This is a book about freedom. We know the word in its political context, but it exists, and achieves its full resonance and majesty, in a psychological form. An exciting life of freedom is different from a merely good or wise or calm life: it is one that can feature novelty, tension, eros, ambition and appreciation. It encompasses a capacity to take risks, to trust and to know how to communicate one's perspective to others. It means allowing oneself to be a little more forthright, joyful, irreverent and unfrightened. This is a book for people who, although living, are only intermittently liberated enough to feel alive, but who are now ready to make meaningful changes.

Contents

1

Others

Learning to lie less often

Our image of liars is so negative, our sense of their motives so dark, our presumption of their primal sinfulness so unyielding, it is no wonder that we generally deny the possibility that we might be liars ourselves.

However, it would be much more honest, and more liberating, to accept that we spend a lot of our lives lying in one way or another, and to grow sympathetic to and curious about the reasons why we do. We tend to focus on the delinquent or semi-criminal aspects of lying – as though deceitfulness always happens in relation to a schoolteacher, an angry father, a gang or the police – and so miss out on its more subtle, everyday psychological varieties in which we, the law-abiding, careful, ostensibly moral majority, are enmeshed.

Despite our disavowals, we are continually lying about some of the following:

Hurts

We lie about the many almost imperceptible hurts that others have inflicted on us but that we lack the vocabulary and the confidence to complain about cleanly. We lie about a range of minor resentments that have made us bitter and irritable and have choked our capacity for warmth and spontaneity. We lie about the number of other humans we are in a (quiet) sulk with.

Guilt

We lie about how sorry we are about certain things we've done, and about how much we long to check in with certain people and apologise, if only we knew that they would greet our confession with a measure of forgiveness.

Tenderness

We lie about how moved we are by many things that busy grown-ups aren't supposed to care too much about: a parent and child walking together hand in hand; the sky at dusk; the face of a stranger in the street; a bad film with a happy ending; a picture of our family decades ago in better times. We disguise the fact that beneath an often confident, brusque adult exterior is a pensive, weepy child.

Anxiety

We lie about how alarming it is to be alive; how frightened we are of the responsibilities we carry; how unsure we are of our path; and how little we understand even at our moments of ostensible authority and competence. In certain moods we might long to utter a despairing 'I don't know …' at much that comes our way.

Sexuality

We lie about a majority of things that turn us on – and about many that really don't but apparently should. We lie about the sensual details that we rehearse in our minds alone late at night and the unfaithful dreams that coexist alongside our public commitments.

Pleasure

We pretend to be having fun skiing and in nightclubs, at the theatre and reading the long novel that won a very important prize. We pretend to love our friends. We lie about how bored we are. We strive not to admit to what we really do like: staying in; eating strange things in a disgusting way alone in the kitchen late at night; plotting revenge; seeing no one; wasting time; buying gadgets; and looking up the fate of ex-lovers and colleagues from long ago.

In the process, without meaning to, we perpetuate a world in which everyone else has to lie along with us. Because everyone refrains from uttering their truths, the price of breaking cover remains impossibly high. We collude in a mass conspiracy to suggest that love, sex, work, family life, friends and holidays unfold in a way we know in our hearts they simply don't. We remain at the dawn of any collective capacity to acknowledge what fundamental parts of life are actually like.

A lack of love holds us back. We are emotional liars because, somewhere during our upbringing, we failed to imbibe a robust sense that we might be acceptable in and of our essence. No one said with enough conviction that we were allowed just to be. We were given convincing lessons in how not to speak our more dangerous thoughts clearly. We became experts at complying. We came to associate being good and normal with being someone else.

How much more interesting it might be if we dared to be a little braver, and conceived of many encounters as opportunities to risk the sharing of new truths. We might realise that our picture of what might happen if we are honest derives from outdated or irrelevant contexts: childhood, the company of narrow-minded schoolmates, obvious bullies, social media … Learning not to lie would not only be of egoistic benefit; our vulnerability would invite, and rehabilitate, that of others. Every confession we could muster would allow our companions to let go of a part of their own loneliness. Every move towards greater honesty would edge us towards a less needlessly isolated and painfully shame-filled world.

Leaning into vulnerability

For many of us, whenever we feel scared, sad, anxious or lonely, the last thing we would think of doing is sharing our distress; a confession threatens to make an already difficult situation untenable. We assume that our best chance of defending ourselves and recovering our self-possession is to say nothing. When we are sad at a gathering of friends, we smile. When we are terrified before a speech, we try to change the subject. When we're asked how we're coping, we say, 'Very well indeed, thank you.' We aren't deliberately out to deceive; we are practising the only manoeuvre we know and trust in response to our vulnerability.

What we fear above all is judgement. We are social creatures who have come to equate being accepted with appearing poised. We assume that we could not explain what is really going on inside us and survive unblemished. In our eyes, the price of safety is the maintenance of a permanent semblance of composure.

However, there might be an alternative to this punishing and isolating philosophy: rather than insisting on our well-being at moments of fear, sadness, anxiety and loneliness, we might actually reveal that things aren't perfect for us; that we're pretty scared right now; that we're finding it hard to talk to people or maintain faith in the future; that we feel anxious and in need of company.

Although we might be alarmed at the prospect of divulging such sentiments, it might help us arrive at some surprising discoveries. We might immediately feel lighter and less oppressed; our connection with those around us might become significantly deeper by sharing more of the turmoil of our inner lives; and, most unexpectedly of all, the revelation of our vulnerability could make us appear stronger rather than weaker in the eyes of others.

Some of our regrettable furtiveness comes from imagining that all disclosures of fear, sadness, anxiety and loneliness must be the same. But this is to ignore a critical difference between a revelation that comes across as an insistent, desperate demand for rescue, and one that frames a problem with an attitude of sober, sad dignity. There is a distinction between begging never to be left alone again and revealing that one has been finding one's evenings a bit quiet of late. There can be a firm and dependable barrier between neediness and vulnerability.

Furthermore, rather than merely not threatening our dignity, revelation may be the very ingredient that enhances it.

However impressive it may superficially be never to show weakness, it is much more impressive to have the courage, psychological insight and self-discipline to talk about one's weaknesses in a boundaried and contained way. It is the mark of a real adult to be able to disclose, with a mixture of aplomb and tact, aspects of one's childlike self: that one has been going through a dreadful time; that one really doesn't want to be here; or that one is very worried about seeming like an idiot. True toughness isn't about maintaining a facade of military robustness, but about an artful negotiation with, and unfrightened acceptance of, one's regressive, dependent aspects.

The ability to pull this off relies on a further piece of maturity: the knowledge that everyone is, at heart, as scared, sad, lonely and anxious as we are. Even if they choose not to reveal this, we can make an empathetic leap of faith that they do so, not because they are fundamentally different and more robustly constituted than us, but because they are scared.

We are all hemmed in by an image of what it means to be a serious adult that doesn't allow us to share our vulnerable reality, and thereby makes us all sick and alienated from ourselves and from one another. We should accept that it is normal to be lonely, even though everyone is meant to have all the friends they need; that it is normal to be sick with worry, even though we're meant to have faith in the future.

In revealing our weaknesses, we are proving we are like our audiences in their true, but hitherto needlessly hidden, reality: we are somersaulting over a social barrier and generously creating a space in which others too may come to feel safe enough to show their fragility and humanity. We can lean into our fears rather than treating them as shameful enemies. Every confession, ably executed, alleviates rather than enforces our burdens. Rather than seeing the world as an entity that we must constantly impress, and our reality as something we must perpetually hide, we can dare to imagine that others would not mind us showing more of our true selves. There might be nothing more generous or impressive we could offer our neighbours than a tranquil disclosure of our feelings of sadness, isolation, worry and existential despair.

Self-assertion

One of the reasons why our lives are harder than they might be is that most of us do not have a firm handle on the art of mature self-assertion; that is, the ability to put forward our interests in a way that seems credible, dignified, serene and effective. Daily we are confronted by challenges to our positions that require us to find a voice: a partner who subtly denies us affection; a colleague who malignly undermines our proposals; a parent who treads on our aspirations.

In response, we tend to behave in two equally unfortunate ways:

1.   We say nothing. After all, who are we to speak; why would anyone listen; how dare we? None of which stops us hating and cursing inside.

2.   We bottle up the toxins until they have built up a head of steam, then let rip a tirade of insults, florid accusations and sulphurous vindictiveness that, at a stroke, destroys the credibility of anything we might be trying to convey and ensures that we can be put in a box labelled 'tyrannical and unhinged'.

Aristotle (384–322 BCE), the first systematic Western explorer of human emotions, suggested that maturity often lies midway between two extremes. His *Nicomachean Ethics* advances a tripartite table outlining ideal forms of behaviour, along with their two characteristically deficient or excessive departures.

Vice from deficiency	Virtuous mean	Vice from excess
Cowardice	*Courage*	Rashness
Shamelessness	*Modesty*	Bashfulness
Pettiness	*Munificence*	Vulgarity

To follow the model in the case of the topic at hand, we might add:

Sulking	Assertion	Rage

At the root of our failures lies one woefully familiar psychological problem: self-hatred. It is because we haven't learnt to love and respect ourselves that we say nothing, believing that we have no right to take our own positions seriously. Associated with this is despair at the possibility of any form of advanced intrahuman understanding. We have no experience of dialogue working out, of someone clearing their throat, apologising for being a nuisance and then calmly and eloquently articulating a point, only for their interlocutor to concede, to thank them for speaking up and to promise to look at things differently in the future. Our inner world is instead populated by shadow images of powerful tyrants who don't listen, and meek serfs with no fair right to exist. Or else, from an associated form of self-suspicion, we rush our lesson and, by making a doomed assault on the integrity of our opponent, essentially prove to ourselves that we knew it would never work out.

It can be exhausting constantly to assert oneself. In the course of a typical day, we will face many moments in which we should speak up properly: politely yet firmly, determinedly yet respectfully. It might have helped if we had received early training, as in one of those childhoods read about in psychology manuals, where a parent gently asks the upset three-year-old: 'Darling, how do you feel about that?' and listens to the answer, rather than telling the child to stop being so silly or attacking them for being inconsiderate after a hard day at the office.

We should see the challenge of mastering assertion as one of the great psychological hurdles. To learn how to assert oneself steadily and graciously might be ranked as a feat no less worthy of celebration (and much more useful) than climbing a mountain or making a fortune.

We should assert ourselves not because it will always work. Indeed, a bit of pessimism can be handy; when we know that people might not understand us, we no longer feel so desperate that they must. We should assert ourselves irrespective of results because it will lend us an important sense of our own agency and strength – and we'll twitch less.

To get us going, right now, we might consider where we are being gently but punishingly trodden on by those around us: people who conveniently and cleverly tell us that it's all our fault, or expect us to do the heavy lifting, or rely on us to smile and put up with their ill temper. Unusually for us, we might properly take on board that life won't go on forever, that we have a right to be here and that there is a small but fair chance of being understood.

For once, rather than saying nothing or shouting, we might wait until we are rested and feeling kind to ourselves and take up a piece of very unfamiliar Aristotelian middle ground, patiently uttering some magical words: *I'd love it if we might have a quick chat at some point, whenever it's convenient. There's something it would feel great to discuss ...*

What everybody really wants

We are often in situations of wanting to help and be kind to others, but of not knowing what they might need. We would like to deepen our connection to them and be of service, yet we lack a real grasp of what we could plausibly offer them. Their minds seem impenetrable; their problems opaque.

At such moments, we would do well to remember that we all possess a superpower – a capacity to give people something we can be sure they require – founded on a primordial and basic insight into human nature: everyone is in deep need of reassurance. Life is a more or less ongoing emergency for everyone. We are invariably haunted by doubts about our value, concerns for our future, shapeless anxiety and dread about things we've done, and feelings of guilt and embarrassment about ourselves. Every day brings new threats to our integrity and, except for very rare moments when we and the world feel solid, there is almost always a background throb of unwellness in our minds. It doesn't matter whether they are old or young, accomplished or starting out, at the top of the tree or struggling to get by, we can count on one thing about anyone we meet: they will be beset by a sense of insecurity and, beneath some excellent camouflage, of desperation.

Perhaps even more than they realise, they will be longing for someone to say something soothing to them; a word to make them feel that they have a right to exist; that we have faith in them; that we know things aren't always easy for them and that – in a vague but real way – we are on their side. It could be a small and barely perceptible remark, but its effect might be critical: that something fascinating they said sticks in our minds; that we know the past few months have not been easy for them; that we've found ourselves thinking of them since our last meeting; that we've noticed and admire the way they go about things; that they deserve a break and are, we can see, carrying so much.

It is easy to mistake reassurance for flattery. But flattery involves a lie to gain advantage, whereas reassurance involves revealing genuine affection – which we normally leave out from embarrassment – in order to bolster someone's ability to endure. We flatter in order to extract benefit; we reassure in order to help. Furthermore, the flatterer tells their prey about their strengths, whereas the reassurer does something infinitely more valuable: they hint that they have seen the weaknesses, but have only tolerance and compassion for them on the basis of sharing fully in comparable examples.

'I think you're going to be fine'; 'Everyone goes through things like these'; 'You have nothing to be ashamed of ...' The words we need to say to reassure aren't new – they can be the most apparently banal of sentences – but we need to keep hearing them because our minds are bad at holding on to their nourishing truths. They are, furthermore, lines that are much more valuable and inclined to stick if someone else addresses them to us than if we try to rehearse them by ourselves.

In 1425, the Florentine artist Masaccio (1401–1428) painted a rendition of Adam and Eve's expulsion from the Garden of Eden on the walls of Florence's Church of Santa Maria del Carmine. We need not believe in any of the supernatural aspects of Genesis to be profoundly moved by the horror-stricken faces of the banished couple. If we are moved, it is because we see a version of an agony that is essentially universal – for all of us have effectively been cast out of the realm of comfort and plenty and obliged to dwell in the lands of uncertainty, humiliation and grief. All of us are beset by woes; all of us are worried to the core, longing for rest and in urgent need of forbearance and gentleness.

Part of the responsibility of living in a time in which few people still believe in divine reassurance is that

Masaccio, *The Expulsion from the Garden of Eden*, c. 1425

Others

each of us can play a part in delivering that reassurance ourselves, to our fellow sufferers, in ordinary moments of our ordinary lives. We do not generally know the details of other people's travails, but we can often be sure of a few things: that they are at some level in a mood of pain and self-suspicion; that certain very significant things will not have gone right; that there will be loneliness, anxiety and shame at play; and that it could therefore make a big difference if we said something, however modest and unoriginal, to bring a little reassurance into their day.

Getting expectations right

In 1905, the Italian economist Vilfredo Pareto (1848–1923) noticed a telling detail about the peas in his garden: 20% of the pea pods seemed to be responsible for yielding 80% of the peas. This struck Pareto because his research into economic productivity had concurrently shown him that 20% of Italians were responsible for generating 80% of the nation's wealth – a figure that later matched what he found to be true in France, Germany and the Netherlands.

The surprisingly widespread applicability of this principle led to the coining of what we now know as the Pareto distribution or, more casually, the 80/20 rule. This can be observed throughout economics and business and states that 80% of effects will come from 20% of causes. For example, in a publishing house, 20% of books will generate 80% of profits; in banking, 80% of profits will come from 20% of clients, and so on.

However salient the 80/20 rule might be in the economic (or horticultural) realm, we remain reluctant to apply it to an area where it might help us most: our personal lives. Here, too, we see a principle akin to the Pareto distribution: 80% of positive elements can be traced back to 20%

of causes. Or, to put it more negatively, 80% of all inputs are likely to be partly or substantially suboptimal.

The reason why we might need to get this principle clear in our minds is that, in practical terms, we live as if the opposite is true. We assume that most of what we will meet with will be pleasant, formative, cheering and redemptive, and that we should budget for disappointment in only a small and exceptional number of cases. Then, when the opposite invariably emerges – when we encounter the frustrating and imperfect nature of existence – we howl with frustration, bitterness and surprise.

To proceed with greater statistical verve and therefore more grace, appreciation and calm, we would be wise to embed the 80/20 rule firmly in our worldview at the dawn of every new day. Some of its principles will look like this:

- Most parts of every city will be ugly, dispiriting and an insult to our longing for order and optimism.

- Most conversations with most people will leave us feeling misunderstood and desolate.

- Most sexual opportunities will not come off.

- Most projects will go wrong.

- Most governments will be corrupt and unimaginative.

- Most of our natural habitats will be destroyed.

- Most days will be sad.

- Most marriages will be intolerable.

- Most glances in the mirror will be a catastrophe.

- Most interactions with our children will be maddening.

- Most books are terrible.

- Most of life will be a waste of time.

Such is the true applicability of the Pareto principle. Far from being a recipe for gloom, heeding it will guarantee that we will not so regularly collide with one of the sharp edges of reality. Of course our work is for the most part wrong; of course our love lives are unhappy; naturally most of the sex we've had has been regrettable; inevitably most people are a waste of our time. Demagogues, advertisers and peddlers of sentimental bromides will constantly urge us to hold out for more, or incite us to be furious that we haven't yet been given it. We should turn away from their aggravating counsel. We have not been singled out for unusual punishment; our lives are following a course that can be observed as much in the operations of a widget factory as in the fertility of plants or the profitability of nations. We need not question our relationships, our employment or our membership of the species. Most of it is no good – and that is exactly as it should be.

But this disgusting truth, once digested, only makes the rare 20% all the more worthy of reverence: those few friends who do open up properly; those occasional nights when it works out; those family members who are undefended and interesting; those days when we feel strong and purposeful. These aren't anything like the norm – nor were they ever meant to be. They are the succulent morsels of the otherwise ineluctably thin harvest we must subsist on, and therefore the parts that we must treasure and draw hope from before darkness returns.

We would be wise to embed the 80/20 rule firmly in our worldview at the dawn of every new day.

2

Self

Learning to be angry

There are many reasons to believe that one of the dominant problems in the world today is an excess of anger. We know all about the very shouty and their antics: their tantrums, their lack of reason, their unwillingness to compromise. Furthermore, this threatens to get a lot worse. We seem locked into a set of dynamics (political, technological, environmental) that promises an ever less patient, ever less serene and ever less forgiving future.

However, it may be more realistic, albeit odd-sounding, to insist on the opposite: that whatever the impression generated by a publicly vocal angry cohort, the far more common problem is a widespread inability to get angry: a failure to know how to effectively mount a complaint; an inarticulate swallowing of frustration; and the bitterness, subterranean acting out and low-level depression that follow from not expressing our rightful sorrows. For every one person who shouts too loudly, there are at least twenty who have unfairly lost their voices.

We are not talking here of delirious rage – the sort that injures innocents and leads nowhere. The point is not to rehabilitate barbarism; it is to make a case for an occasional capacity to speak up, with dignity and poise, in order to correct a reasoned sense that something isn't right and that those around us need to take our opposing perspective on board.

As a rule, we are hopeless at being angry, and from the very nicest of motives. In part this stems from a belief in the complexity of situations and the minds of other people, which undercuts enthusiasm for anything that smacks of self-righteousness or pride. We tell ourselves, in relationships or at work, that others must have good reasons for behaving as they do, that they must be essentially kind and good, and that it would be an insult to their efforts to raise our hand about a problem that we surely don't understand entirely.

We tend to import our modesty from childhood. It is a privilege to allow a child to manifest their frustration – and not all parents are game. Some are keen on having a 'good' baby. They let the infant know that being 'naughty' isn't funny and that this isn't a family where children are allowed to run rings around the adults. Difficult moods and tantrums, complaints and rages are not to be part of the story. This certainly ensures short-term compliance; however, paradoxically, preternaturally good behaviour is often a precursor to bad feelings and, in extremes, mental unwellness in adulthood. Feeling loved enough that one can tell parental figures to sod off and occasionally fling something (soft) across the room belongs to health; truly mature parents have rules and allow their children (sometimes) to break them.

Otherwise, there is a species of inner deadness that comes from having been forced to be too good too soon and to resign one's point of view without a flicker of self-defence. In relationships, this might mean a tendency to get taken for a ride for many years – not in terms of outright abuse (though that too), but the kind of low-level humiliation that seems the lot of people who can't make a fuss. At work, an unwavering concern for politeness, empathy and gentleness may end up providing the perfect preconditions for being walked all over.

We should try to relearn the neglected art of politely being a pain. The danger of those who have never shouted is that they might, in compensation, end up screaming. That isn't the point either. The goal is a firm but self-possessed protest: 'Excuse me, but you are ruining what's left of my life'; 'I'm so sorry, but you are cauterising my chances of happiness'; 'I beg your pardon, but this is enough …'

We think a lot about going on holiday and trying new activities. There is a lot of enthusiasm for learning other languages and attempting foreign dishes. But true exoticism and adventure may lie closer to home: in the emotional sphere, and in the courage and originality required to give contained anger a go, perhaps tonight, after supper. We have the speeches written in our heads already. There is likely to be a spouse, a parent, a colleague or a child who hasn't heard enough from us for far too long, and with whom it would be of incalculable benefit to our heart rate and our emotional and physical constitution to have a word. The timid always imagine that anger might destroy everything good. Because their childhoods encouraged them to, they overlook the fact that anger can also be a fertiliser from which something a lot less bitter and a lot more alive can emerge.

Escaping the shadow of a parent

When we think about children living under the shadow of a parent, we tend to imagine the offspring of especially distinguished, notorious or wealthy people. Whatever they might go on to do by their own initiative, these children will always interest the world primarily as the son or daughter of X or Y. Far into their lives, their own personalities and aspirations will pale next to the key fact about them: that they are the child of John Lennon or Charles Darwin, that Mum was Marie Curie or Dad the inventor of the telephone.

John Lennon and his son Julian Lennon, c. 1960

However, such high-profile cases should not distract us from the universality of the theme in question: our parents need not have written 'Imagine' or discovered the theory of evolution in order to cast some very large shadows across our lives. These shadows might not be generated by money or fame, but by the strength and complexity of their personalities, which threaten to derail the sane and autonomous emergence of our own.

It is not only being the child of Elvis Presley or the Duke of Wellington that is problematic; it could be being the son or daughter of anyone with an immovable story in their head about who we need to be in order to deserve their love; any parent who leaves us longing for their approval through their inconsistent and unreliable affection; any parent who leaves us a legacy of guilt around sex or a worry that we have abandoned them by getting on with our lives; any parent who subtly signals that it would be better if we didn't succeed in love or could accept that our sibling is truly the worthwhile and good one.

An emotional shadow comprises a panoply of (normally secret) commands about what will be required of a child to warrant affection and, metaphysically speaking, a place on Earth. Rather than a kingdom or a fortune, the parent hands down a set of invisible rules: you should never rival your mother or father's achievements; you must never be happier than I was; you must love people who will deny you security; you should not think of yourself as a man or woman in the true sense; you must worry perpetually about money; you must forever feel that what you've done isn't enough ... Such are the hidden commandments that one generation slips unnoticed into the psyches of the next.

As a result, without fully seeing the contours of the shadow we operate under, in one relationship after another, we may be taken advantage of or wind up unable to feel comfortable receiving affection. At work, we may take early retirement from our real ambitions, telling ourselves, despite objective evidence to the contrary, that we don't have the talent required. Getting angry is impossible. We don't allow ourselves to be too amusing or too excited. We feel guilty every time we spend money on ourselves. We're living half the life that should be our due.

At the same time, typically, we think a lot more about our parents than we should. We are still scared of their anger, even though they might have been dead for twenty years. We fret about their well-being, as if they were in effect the child. We worry constantly that they might be sad or feeling rejected without us. We long for their approval and have them as our implicit audience for all our efforts. Our memory of their value system hampers us whenever we try to enjoy ourselves. Being mildly depressed feels safer and more respectful.

An emotional shadow is always, ultimately, created by blackmail. The deal is as follows: do as we want, or we will quietly choke off a supply of love; follow our way, or you must suffer and fail. There may be a lot of love from the shadow-throwing parent, but not of the sort that has the recipient's authentic autonomy at heart. Of course, it shouldn't matter who the child chooses to marry, what job they go for or how they bring up their own child in turn. To be a good parent is willingly to cede control, to let oneself be forgotten, never to loom too large in the child's imagination; not to present a massive obstacle to growth or achievement; not to become an object of worry or pity; not to be a source of fear or alarm; not to be the patron of self-esteem; to realise that offering someone protection never means having the right to control their identity and psychic functioning. The greatest gift of a parent is that they should be kind enough to give us the right to forget them.

To liberate ourselves at last, we need an adolescence. The full grandeur and seriousness of the concept of adolescence is too often obscured by its association with grumpiness and acne. But something very serious is at stake in this phase: permission to define oneself afresh and get far out of the shadow. Many of us, unknown to ourselves, managed not to have an adolescence at fifteen. There wasn't enough love to dare to. Not every parent is mature enough to allow themselves to be hated and belittled. We may be close to menopause or past retirement before we have the courage finally to dip a toe into adolescence.

In this process, it helps to talk to someone else about our family. The one thing about shadows is that they don't like attention. They would prefer if no one got to hear the story and the secret rules; these start to seem ridiculous and questionable once one puts them into words with an unbiased and kindly observer (it can help if he or she is about the same age as one's parents).

Tricky parents function as ghosts who can only be laid to rest by illumination. Our growth requires that we confront something abysmally sad: that we weren't loved as we might have been and that, as a result, we are far from properly free. We might have wasted a big part of our lives in a straitjacket not of our own making. Parents can expect a lot from us, but they don't have a right to our identities. At the same time, more clearly than ever, we can see that the point of true parental love is not to produce a clone, but to give encouragement to an autonomous new member of the human race – something we may now slowly be on the way to becoming.

On friendliness to strangers

Many of us, even the very kind ones, have a habit of walking through the world wearing a distinctly uncongenial and surly expression. If someone secretly photographed us on our way to the station or back from the shops, we might wince at our appearance: how stern our resting face is; how guarded we look; how misanthropic we seem. This could pain us in part because we know this is not the whole story. Our outward manner is at odds with a warmer, kinder, more vulnerable and sociable self that we know also exists and that seeks – largely in vain and often rather clumsily – to find expression. We are curmudgeons who harbour thwarted longings for new friendships.

However, it should not be surprising that we have ended up so walled off and uninclined to share ourselves with strangers. Without realising it, we have been given long training in our attitudes. We have been told a lot about the world outside our insulated, predictable routines. We know that the stranger is, as a rule, pretty dangerous, has little to teach us, is likely to be sinister and may well be demented. Admittedly, we have generally not done our own research; we have let others find out for us. On this score, the media's conclusions are refreshed on our screens every hour of every day: others are to be feared; the unknown is to be avoided; the world (outside our close-knit circle) is mad.

However, the reality is that, despite the surface evidence, strangers are always likely to resemble someone we already know well: us. Beneath the unfamiliar exterior, the distinctive accent, the alien occupation, the unexplored age or social bracket, the stranger is often merely a version of ourselves, the same essential human matter squeezed through a slightly different social and psychological mould:

- The stranger is pained by regrets.

- The stranger is wracked by longings.

- The stranger, despite their impassive appearance, craves love and fellowship.

- The stranger is lonely.

- The stranger loves to laugh, but hasn't been silly and playful in a long time.

- The stranger was once a baby.

- The stranger might want to say hello.

The places where we most often see strangers – crowded shopping streets, airless subway carriages, airport concourses – tend not to lend plausibility to the above suggestions; they reinforce a message that others must be unfathomable and eerie. Yet feeling at home in the world relies to some extent on going beyond or to the side of the available evidence, refusing to be cowed by surface details and insisting on a theoretical capacity to locate the humanity of all beneath the outer casing.

This is the trick of that guileless artist of the everyday we call the friendly person. They take an attitude of basic goodwill out into unknown spaces. They assume that the stranger will be open to a smile, a reflection on the season, a supportive glance or an unobtrusive greeting. They will suspect that beneath a surly manner, the assistant might be aching to share something of themselves; that, even when there are only a few minutes available, it will be possible to say something heart-warming to a colleague or an official; that one can empathise across the barriers of age, class and profession.

Shyness has its insightful dimensions: it is infused with an awareness that we might be bothering someone with our presence; it is based upon an acute sense that a stranger could be dissatisfied or discomfited by us.

The shy person is touchingly alive to the dangers of being a nuisance. Someone with no capacity for shyness is a scary possibility; they operate with a dismaying attitude of entitlement. They are friendly only because they haven't considered the possibility that the other person might have a disenchanted view of them.

However, we often pay a heavy price for our reserve around people who might have opened their hearts to us, if only we had known how to manifest our own benevolence. We cling too jealously to our province. The pimply boy doesn't discover that he and the high school beauty share a taste in humour and similarly painful relationships with their fathers; the middle-aged lawyer never unearths a shared love of rockets with the neighbour's eight-year-old son. Races and ages continue not to mingle, to their collective detriments. Shyness is a touching yet ultimately excessive and unwarranted way of feeling unique.

Guessing what might be going on in the hearts of strangers is a fundamental move of the artist. Without being able to know for sure, these characters bravely and beautifully presume that they might know a key secret bit of you – because they know the key secret bits of themselves. The American poet E.E. Cummings (1894–1962) didn't wait to be introduced and didn't worry about all the ways in

Shyness is a touching yet ultimately excessive and unwarranted way of feeling unique.

which you and he were not going to be identical. He assumed that you would understand one or two important things – and he more or less got it right, which is why his poem 'since feeling is first' (1926) continues to resonate:

> since feeling is first
> who pays any attention
> to the syntax of things
> will never wholly kiss you;
>
> wholly to be a fool
> while Spring is in the world

Cummings' talent was a species of confidence; a way of imagining a commonality between your deep self and his.

With some of that same confidence, we should dare more often to guess at the contents of the hearts of strangers. Without being presumptuous, we might offer a new person some of the reassurance we long for. We might show them a vulnerable part of ourselves; we could express warmth and curiosity; we might go out into the world and share a few tentative thoughts with a stranger and trust that they might one day be a friend.

Dealing with depression

Almost half of us will suffer from depression at some point in our lives, but the condition remains badly misunderstood and therefore often poorly treated. At the heart of our collective difficulty with depression is a confusion about what it actually is – in particular, how it can be distinguished from a state all of us know very well and with which it shares a number of similarities: sadness. We often unwittingly apply to cases of depression assumptions drawn from an understanding of sadness, and therefore end up suffering far more than we should.

On the surface, there are similarities between those who are sad and those who are depressed. Both groups cry; both withdraw from the world; both complain of listlessness and a sense of alienation from their normal lives. But there is one categorical difference between depression and sadness: the sad person knows what they are sad about; the depressed person doesn't.

Sad people can, without difficulty, tell us what is troubling them. They are sad that their pet died, or that they lost their job, or that their friends are unkind. The depressed person is not capable of doing this. They may be tearful, but they cannot conclusively identify what has drained life of meaning for them: they simply say it has no meaning per se. They aren't depressed about X or Y as one might be sad about X or Y. They are simply depressed.

The inability of the depressed person to account for their mood can lay them open to unwarranted charges of faking, malingering or exaggerating. Friends looking for a solvable problem can end up frustrated by lack of progress. When pushed, the depressed person might latch on to rather odd or minor-sounding issues to account for their state: they might complain that there is no point going to work because the Earth is due to be absorbed by the Sun in 7.5 billion years. Or they might insist that life lacks all meaning because they've broken a glass and everything is now completely hopeless.

One often hears that if depression has no obvious psychological causes, the problem must be bound up with an imbalance in brain chemistry, which can be treated with pills. This is an idea that greatly appeals to the pharmaceutical industry, but also to worried families, schools and employers who crave rapid and cost-effective solutions.

However, there is another approach to depression that, although slower and more arduous, may be much more effective in the long term. This stems from insights drawn from psychotherapy, the discipline that arguably has been able to understand depression better than any other. The basic premise of psychotherapy is that the depressed person is not depressed *for no reason*; there is a reason. They are distressed about *something*, but that something is proving difficult to take on board, and has therefore been pushed into the outer zones of consciousness, from where it wreaks havoc on the whole person, prompting boundless feelings of nihilism.

For depressives, realising what they are concretely upset about would be too devastating. Therefore, they unconsciously choose to remain dead to everything as opposed to very distraught about something. Depression is sadness that has forgotten its true causes – forgotten because remembering may generate overwhelming, untenable feelings of pain and loss.

What might these true causes be? Perhaps that we have married the wrong person, or that our sexuality isn't what we once believed, or that we are furious with a parent for their lack of care in childhood. In order to preserve a fragile peace of mind, one then 'chooses' (although that may sound more willed than it is in reality) to be depressed rather than to have a realisation. We pick unceasing numbness as protection against dreadful insight.

To make things even more difficult, the depressed person typically does not consciously feel that they are lacking insight. They are not aware of a gap in their self-understanding. Furthermore, they are often taught to assume that they are 'just depressed', as one might just be physically ill – a verdict that can appeal as much to the pharmaceutical industry as to certain people close to the depressed person with an interest in insights remaining buried.

There is another key difference between sadness and depression. Sad people are grief-stricken about something out in the world, but they aren't necessarily sad about themselves; their self-esteem is unaffected by their grief. Conversely, depressed people characteristically feel wretched about themselves and are full of self-recrimination, guilt, shame and self-loathing paranoia that may, at tragic extremes, culminate in suicidal thoughts.

For psychotherapy, the origins of this self-hatred lie in anger due for, but unable to be directed towards, someone else in the world, which has then turned against the sufferer. Wrathful feelings that should have gone outwards – towards a partner who is relentlessly defensive and denies one sex, or a parent who humiliated one in childhood – are driven back onto the sufferer and start to attack them. The feeling 'X has let me down horribly' turns into the unpleasant but in some ways more bearable 'I'm an unworthy and unbearable wretch.' One becomes self-hating as a defence against the risks of hating someone else.

Also worth noting is that, in many cases, depression is associated with an apparently opposite mood, a euphoric state termed 'mania'; hence the term 'manic depressive'. The mania in question looks, from a distance, something like happiness, just as depression can resemble sadness. But in one area, the relationship between mania and happiness is identical to that between depression and sadness. The common element is a disavowed self-knowledge. In mania, one is euphoric but cannot go into one's own deep mind and discover its bitter truths. This explains one of the leading characteristics of manic people: their habit of being in flight from themselves, talking too fast about nothing, over-exercising, working continuously or spending too much – all as an escape from a submerged grief, rage and loss.

It is from this kind of diagnosis that a suggested cure emerges. What people in depression need above all is a chance to arrive at insight. For this, they will tend to need a supportive and patient listener. They may also benefit from temporary use of medication, if used appropriately, to lift their mood just enough so that they can endure a conversation. However, the assumption is not that brain chemistry is where the problem either begins or ends; the despair is caused by an undigested, unknown and unresolved trauma. Far from needing to be taken through reasons to trust that life is beautiful, depressives must be allowed to feel and to remember specific damage, and to be granted a fundamental sense of the legitimacy of their emotions. They need to be allowed to be angry, and for the anger to settle on the right, awkward targets.

The goal in treating depression is to move a sufferer from feeling limitlessly despairing to mourning the loss of something in particular: the last twenty years, a marriage, a hope that one would be loved by one's father, a career … However agonising the insight and mourning might be, these must always be preferable to allowing loss to contaminate the totality of one's perspective. There are plenty of dreadful things in every life, which is why it is normal to feel sad on a regular basis. But there are also a sufficient number of things that remain beautiful and hopeful, so long as one has been allowed to understand and know one's pain and anger and adequately mourn one's losses.

3

Relationships

Arguing more nakedly

In long-term relationships, we are likely to spend up to 10% of our time in the intoxicating and all-consuming business of arguing. Each argument will seem to be uniquely about itself. It will have its distinct flashpoint, features, injustices, stupidities and what to us appear to be self-evident truths that the partner is blithely resisting: the absurdity of proposing to leave at 7.23 p.m. when we had both agreed – only two hours ago – that we would leave no later than 7.10 p.m.; the idiocy of telling a younger son he could have extra screen time when we'd already explained to him that he'd breached his limit; the insult of the partner laughing aloud at our sister-in-law's cheap jibe against us at the family reunion ...

Faced with such offences, we dig in like eager and well-paid lawyers, crash investigators or detectives. We marshal evidence. We say that on the basis of this or that, they are obviously going to have to rethink their line and surrender to our perspective. The first round may begin peacefully enough, but the urgency and annoyance stand to increase as the second and third rounds unfold, each team adding a little vengeance and irritation to their proclamations. Sometimes, with the logic of the argument so stubbornly resisted by the other party, voices will be raised, faces will flush, someone (whom we have named in our will and to whom we have otherwise given our lives) may be called a c*** or a b******, a door might be slammed and a gloom could descend that will take a good two days to clear.

Such rigmaroles are so shameful and dispiriting that we tend not to mention their entrails to others – and others in turn keep quiet about their squabbles to us, deepening our feelings of isolation and embarrassment. We say that 'we've had a bit of a tiff' or are 'going through a bad patch' in lieu of confessing openly that the person we love appears (sometimes at least) to have substantially ruined our lives.

The great error we make is to assume that the way to fix an argument is to attempt to reach an objective truth that, once brought out into the open, can neutralise the force of the fierce offence we feel. However, there is an unfortunate and somewhat paradoxical aspect of arguments in relationships: it doesn't really matter what the truth is; it's by the by who has the stronger case; it's irrelevant who can 'win'.

Behind, or beneath, an argument, there is only ever one thing we really want from our partners: to know we are loved. We are arguing so bitterly not because a client has hired us in a courtroom, but because we are emotionally in pain, because the relationship has forced us to make ourselves vulnerable in front of another person on whom we depend. Beneath our furious eloquence, we are longing for reassurance. We are calling them a c*** in lieu of asking them tearfully if they still love us and why, in that case, they have hurt us so much.

Rather than dwell tirelessly on the surface complaints, we might learn to cut straight to the emotional substratum of the situation and raise one of six possible objections to the partner:

1. I feel you don't value me.

2. I feel abandoned.

3. I feel not good enough.

4. I feel you are trying to control me.

5. I feel you're not accepting who I really am.

6. I feel unseen and unheard.

If the words seem too hard to utter, we might simply paste the list to the fridge door and point mutely to it at the height of a dispute. Rather than try to win a proxy managerial battle over scheduling or bedtimes, we might immediately disclose the emotional explanation for our upset: 'When you are late for something we'd agreed on, I feel unseen and unheard'; 'When you contradict me in front of my family, I feel abandoned.'

By a grievous logic, it often seems that the only way to feel safe is to punch back, when in love we will be much safer (that is, much more likely to be a recipient of affection and atonement) if we manage calmly to reveal our wound to its (usually unwitting) perpetrator. The best response is not to make ourselves more impregnable, but to dare to be a little less defended.

Differences of opinion between partners may crop up over anything, but arguments – the sort of heated matches that end in slammed doors and insults – are only ever about one thing: the anxiety of being excessively vulnerable before someone we adore and can't control. It may look like a fight over scheduling or childcare, but really it's a fight about the terror of emotional abandonment. If we kept this idea in mind, we might save ourselves so much time in legalistic point scoring – possibly four hours a week or more that could be put to use gardening, helping the aged or learning a foreign language. There would be so much less to shout about, and so many more exciting things to get on with.

The stranger you've been living alongside for years

After we have been living alongside a partner for a few years, there is no more common response than a feeling of intense (though normally very privately held) boredom. However intriguing they might have been at the start, and however accomplished they remain in theory, we tend to end up in the unfortunate position of knowing most of their anecdotes, of being able to predict their responses, of having seen them from every angle and of being left to smile wanly at their now awkwardly familiar set of jokes. Without meaning to be disloyal, our eyes develop a tendency to drift. We can fall for faces we glimpse momentarily on the subway or in the grocery store, and that seem to harbour all the charm and depths of the unknown. Haunted by an impression of mesmerising but unattainable mystery, we become irritable and ungrateful towards the one person who has opted to spend their life in our company.

It is understandable that we should seek novelty in love; our characteristic error is to believe that this must mean we should seek out a new partner. Restless, we miss out on a critically redemptive idea: that the person we have been with for so long, perhaps for many years, is in fact a stranger. Paradoxically, they are a stranger precisely because our physical proximity and familiar joint routines have lulled us into assuming that we know them thoroughly already, and that dissuades us from continuing to bring to bear on them the kind of searching intelligence we might apply to someone new. It is our assumption of knowledge that deals our curiosity a fatal blow and encourages us to feel listless and dissatisfied where we should more fairly remain inquisitive and enchanted.

In the early days, we are helped by the obviousness of our ignorance. We understand that we need to get to know the basics: the structure of their family; their educational and career trajectories; their friendships and travels; their cultural tastes and domestic habits. But at a certain point, astonishingly, we stop. We believe we have done enough; we trust that it might be possible to understand someone in the course of 150 hours or so of chat. And then we shift to practicalities, to reflections on the news, the latest things at work and when someone might be coming to check the boiler. We no longer expect big disclosures and cease to prepare or hunt for them. Our partial knowledge functions as a dispiriting reason not to ask for more. We fail to extend to our partner the basic insight we all know from within: that we are never quite done with understanding the mind; that only a tiny portion of its endless canyons is ever illuminated by reason (and therefore available to oneself, let alone another person); and that we can orbit consciousness for years without ever grasping more than a fraction of its content. We confuse seeing our lover every day with understanding their soul.

Our neglect of the complexities of our partner mirrors our jaded attitude to the world around us more generally. We are no less lacking in curiosity about our country, our city or our own home. In these cases too we look around and see only banality and the mundane, and are prone to long for the obviously exotic and foreign instead.

One counter to this settled ingratitude lies in certain works of art that contain coded pleas for us to notice the intricacy and beauty of overlooked aspects of the everyday. Over the centuries, artists have used their talents to say what in effect amounts to: 'Notice the astonishing sunlight as it hits the top of the trees, the delicacy of the water rippling by the shore, the solemnity of the fog hugging the landscape at dusk ...' They challenge us to notice afresh what we think we have already seen.

For example, the Impressionist artist Édouard Manet in 1880 looked afresh at a bunch of asparagus, looking at the spring vegetable with the appreciative sensitivity of a young child or a Martian newly landed on the planet. Where we might have been prepared to recognise only dull white stalks, the artist observed and then reproduced vigour, colour and individuality, recasting this humble foodstuff as a sacramental object through which we might recover faith in life more broadly.

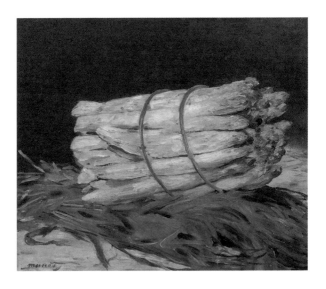

Édouard Manet, *A Bunch of Asparagus*, 1880

In the spirit of Manet, we might turn to consider our partner as if they too were an alien, wondrous object worthy of sustained appreciation and study. We might begin by inviting them out on a date and talk to them as if we knew almost nothing about them – which, it turns out, we don't. With newfound modesty, we could consider all the topics that we had skated over far too quickly at the start and then never bothered to return to. What was their relationship with their mother like? What did their parents fail to understand about them? In what ways were they misunderstood as a child? Over the main course we might turn to their careers: what gives their work purpose? In what areas do they lack confidence? Where do they see their essential strengths? We could then move on to their aspirations: what remains exciting for them? What would they be sad if they never achieved? What are their hopes for the future? What, in their eyes, is the meaning of their life?

Later in the evening, in a similar vein, we could remember that we know next to nothing about them sexually, even if we have made love to them hundreds of times and slept many thousands of nights with them: where do they most like to be touched? What turns them on? What are their most intense fantasies? We could put aside the veil of partial knowledge that has prevented us from seeing them and unclothe them properly as if for the very first time. And we might do this not once, but as a regular exercise to remind us of the ongoing mystery of someone we could only ever think of as familiar by error and hubris.

With such techniques in mind, we stand to recognise something at once alarming and relieving: we don't need to go out and find a new lover in order to recover a sense of excitement. We don't need to learn to look at new people with jaded eyes; we need new eyes to look afresh at the familiar world around us – and, in particular, the total stranger in the bed beside us.

Learning to lay down boundaries

One of the reasons why our lives might be less than they could be is that we have missed out on an awkward-sounding but critical art, whose absence we may never even have noticed: that of laying down boundaries.

Laying down a boundary involves informing those around us – colleagues, parents, children, lovers – of a given set of objectively reasonable things that we are going to require in order to feel respected and happy, while doing so in a way that conveys confidence, self-possession, warmth and a mixture of kindness and strength.

Those who can successfully lay down boundaries will tell their small child that, even though they love them very much, once this game is over, Mummy or Daddy is not going to play another round and it will be time to go upstairs for hair washing, and biting or kicking is not the answer, as we've discussed before. The good boundary-builder will wait until everyone is well rested to tell their partner that, although they appreciate them taking the initiative in many areas, when it comes to their own family, they want to be left in charge, and therefore don't think it was right for the partner to call up their mother-in-law without warning in order to arrange the forthcoming holidays. At work, the boundaried manager will tell their new hire that, although they want to be supportive where possible, it simply is not their role to complete schedules or manage budgets for others.

However, because most of us have not been educated in this byway of emotional maturity, the boundaries are either non-existent or else get thrown up in a jerky and destructive manner; as the technical language has it, we are either too compliant or too rigid. Therefore, Mummy or Daddy might never say that they've had enough of the game and, even when wilting, will play on late into the night, ensuring that their child will be exhausted and cross the next day, as well as craving the security that comes from knowing that their grown-up is 'grown up' enough to say no. (If there's one thing we crave more than that our wishes are granted, it's someone responsible enough to resist granting them all.) In a relationship, we might never explain what we require in order to feel content, and therefore either store up our resentments (and may therefore grow unable to have sex) or else burst into unexplained rages that exhaust our partner's capacity for love. At work, meanwhile, we might develop a reputation as a friendly pushover or as an unreasonable tyrant who it becomes fun to try to evade.

Those who can't lay down boundaries have invariably not had their own boundaries respected in their early lives. Someone didn't allow them to say when they were unhappy with a genuinely difficult situation; someone didn't care much about their hurt feelings or distinctive hopes. Someone insinuated that being good meant falling in line, always and immediately. No one modelled the skill of winning, graceful objection. Now, when the time comes to make a request of others, three powerful anxieties bedevil the boundary-less person:

- If I speak up, they will hate me.

- If I speak up, I will become a target for retribution.

- If I speak up, I will feel like a horrible person.

Although such fears manifest themselves as unquestionable certainties, they are amenable to gentle probing. People almost never hate those who make polite and reasonably framed demands; in fact, they tend to respect and like them a little more. They feel they are in the presence of a mature and kindly authority that appears worthy of their time, as well as seeming rare and somewhat thrilling. Frustrating someone's wishes does not have to be evidence of selfishness; it may signal a noble concern for another's long-term well-being and flourishing. One can adore someone, wish them the very best, have the kindest intentions towards them and still, diplomatically yet decisively, tell them no.

An alternative response to building boundaries is the habit of throwing up walls topped with razor wire ringed by machine gun turrets, or a tendency to become swiftly and gratingly defensive. The manically defensive person too is labouring under a set of unfortunate misapprehensions:

- Everyone is trying to hurt them.

- No one will listen unless they hit back with immense force.

- Their needs can never truly be met.

However, the alternative to lacking boundaries is not violent defensiveness. We should not let boundary building be undermined by its most zealous practitioners; there is always a means to make a sound case without reaching for a weapon.

It is notable that the problem of boundary building is particularly acute not so much around strangers but in intimate life. We may be able to fight our corner with people we care little about (the person at the car rental desk, the tax official), but the problem comes when we are dealing with someone who we know loves us and who we have allowed into our emotional inner sanctum. It is as if, in a deep part of our minds, we cannot reconcile the notion that someone might at once be genuinely caring *and* capable of betraying our best interests. We find it hard to be simultaneously intimate and, always, a touch vigilant. What should help us to absorb that eventuality is to remember that, just as we can say no and still be kind, so another can have harmed us and yet remain, in their essence, *good*.

It takes a little self-confidence and courage to be able to notice just how bad we may be at the art of boundary-laying. We may have spent a large chunk of our lives already in an essentially passive relationship to everyday infringements by people close to us. But we are not a piece of helpless flotsam on the river of others' wishes; we have agency, direction and – as it were – a rudder. The price to pay for affection is not compliance. We can gradually take on board an implausible-sounding but redemptive notion: we can prove loveable and worthy of respect and, at the same time, when the occasion demands it, utter a warm but definitive 'no'.

The benefits of insecurity

We tend to assume that the best foundations for a good shared life for a couple lie in making an explicit commitment (probably in front of 200 guests and a large cake) to staying together for the very long term: the more we are guaranteed that someone is going to stay with us pretty much indefinitely, the more we can mobilise our best sides and bring our virtues into play.

However, it might pay to consider an alternative and more paradoxical truth: that a healthy dose of insecurity, of wondering whether the other person truly is duty-bound to stay with us forever and vice versa, might be the ingredient that helps us to be better people, to curtail our more self-indulgent sides and to conduct a more flourishing and valuable relationship. Rather than drowning in insecurity, might we not benefit from emphasising and embracing the fragility of our alliance? Rather than a solemn promise that this is forever, might not the most romantic move (in the sense of what is most likely to enhance and sustain love) be a gentle reminder that we might not be an item by next month?

Insecurity sounds unromantic, but one of its major consequences is the possibility of appreciating why we remain together. So long as we believe that we are irrevocably attached, there is no need to feel grateful for a partner's positive sides or to notice their contributions to our welfare. All these are merely a given, part of the fabric of our emotional reality.

It tells us something of the importance of remembering endings that, for centuries, the most fitting piece of interior decoration for a prosperous person's study was thought to be a skull: a real skull, with ghoulish eye sockets and anguished-looking rotten teeth, so that, as merchants or politicians went about their business, they would never be far from a reminder that every second was of value.

Philippe de Champaigne, *Still-Life with a Skull vanitas*, c. 1671

Relationships

We should have our own skulls around love. For much of our romantic lives, however much the intellectual idea is in place, the reality of love's demise remains only in shadow. It is not a concrete, powerful conviction that courses through us every hour. And although this allows us to bring a reassuring degree of innocence to our plans, it is also the breeding ground for emotional complacency. We may not experience ourselves as inured to our partners, but in the lackadaisical way we often approach them, we implicitly behave as if waking up every day next to them has privately been guaranteed to us by an all-knowing god, rather than as a gift daily offered to us by a fellow option-rich mortal.

Another paradoxical-sounding result of good insecurity is that it reduces the dangers of bitterness and suppressed irritation. So long as we have no option but to stay, a lot of what we are unhappy about may end up hidden, because our complaints have nowhere to go. We can lose the right to have our needs listened to and respected because both sides know that there is no alternative. Our threats have no ammunition in them; we can stamp our feet like impotent emperors. However, when the relationship is fruitfully insecure, we can confidently state our problems with how things are, both sides knowing that our words mean something. And, of course, our partner can in turn make their dissatisfactions plain to us with equal force. We are importing into the depths of our relationships some of the qualities that attended their fragile beginnings: the empathy, the care and the effort to be pleasant. In a state of constant insecurity, the important focus becomes on why it might be exciting or helpful or interesting to stay together; it turns the decision to remain in a couple into a loving, authentic choice rather than a prison to which no one has the key.

It may sound kind, but we are doing another person, and ourselves, a disservice when we promise that we will never leave them. There is nothing more likely to usher in the death of love than the whispered words: *I will always be with you*. We can appreciate the touching sentiment, but we should never let ourselves become trapped in its many asphyxiating consequences.

Along the way, insecurity is also sexually enticing. There is nothing more devastating to sexual self-confidence than our knowledge that we could never appeal to anyone but our partner, or that they have themselves grown invisible to the rest of humanity. We want what others want – which might include slipping our hand inside our momentarily intriguingly distant partner's top. It is when our lover spots us flirting with an unknown person at a party, or when we are forced to note how appealing they are to an audience of strangers that sex will once again be more than a chore. It is not for nothing that the most intense sex that long-established couples ever have is right after a furious argument; that is, after a vivid encounter with the independence and fiery competence of someone they had for too long mistaken for furniture. Feeling jealous is simultaneously the most abhorrent emotion and the one most necessary to galvanise us back into erotic life.

To get the benefits of insecurity, leaving has to be a real possibility. Our readiness to quit can't be uttered as a hollow threat blurted out when we are fed up or angry, if both sides know that we would in reality struggle to pack our own suitcase or operate our bank account. It has to be built upon a mature realisation that it would be plausible for us to be on our own; that we could manage our own finances, construct a decent social life and do the grocery shopping by ourselves.

If there are children involved, it is sometimes argued that they need to know that we will never part in order to have the security to develop without anxiety. But this is a misreading of the benefits of eternal promises. Maintaining insecurity in a couple is not about trying not to be together; it is about understanding the best preconditions for staying.

Therefore, one of the most constructive things we might do in the pursuit of a more fulfilling relationship is to look in an estate agent's window and work out, realistically, how we could get an apartment for one. With a secure, positive sense of our own capacity for independence, we would learn to see our relationship not as the union of two desperate, option-less people, unable and too frightened to face life alone, but of two creative, independent, sexually alluring individuals who could have an interesting time apart but have chosen to take real pleasure in being with one another to enrich themselves and grow – at least for the time being ...

Untragic endings

News of the end of relationships tends to be greeted with deep solemnity in our societies; it is hard not to think of a break-up except in terms of a minor tragedy. People will offer condolences as they might at a funeral. This in turn reflects an underlying philosophy of love: we are taught that the natural and successful outcome of any love story should be to seek to remain with a person until their death or our own, and, by implication, that any break-up must be interpreted as a failure governed by overwhelming hostility on one or both sides.

However, there is another scenario in which we understand that we are separating not because our relationship has gone badly but because it has gone well; it is ending because it has succeeded. Rather than breaking up with feelings of hurt, bitterness, regret and guilt, we are parting with a sense of mutual gratitude and joint accomplishment.

This counter-intuitive but real possibility comes from having kept a crucial question in mind throughout our time together: what is this relationship for? The enquiry may feel negative; we imagine it being asked in a disillusioned tone of voice. But it can, and should, be asked positively and eagerly, with the aim of finding a good answer that goes to the heart of love.

Normally, we imagine love as a kind of ownership: full of admiration, two people agree to buy one another as they might a static, beguiling object. But there is another, more dynamic and less hidebound way to interpret love: as a particular kind of education. In this view, a relationship comprises a mutual attempt to learn from and teach something to another person. We are drawn to our partners because we want to be educated by them and vice versa; we love them because we see in them things that we long for but that are missing in us; we aspire to grow under the tutelage of love.

For example, a partner might at the outset have been confident but gentle – a combination that, until we met them, seemed impossible. Or they knew how to laugh at themselves, while we were too withheld and solemn to do so. Or they had a practical competence that we found delightful and moving precisely because it was lacking in us. We could accurately say in such cases that the purpose of the relationship was to teach us confidence, or gentleness, or how to laugh at our own idiocy, or how to become more dexterous – or a thousand other qualities depending on who we both are. The point is that there will be some specific and important things we need to do together that define what the relationship is for.

By being with the partner, by intertwining our lives, by listening to them, even by being criticised or nagged by them, we will gradually be able to internalise what they have to teach us. But there may come a point where we have absorbed as much from them as we can. Thanks to our partner, we are more mature beings than we were when we got together. We're more balanced and wiser; they've helped us to become a little more like the people we always wished to be.

Precisely because our relationship has had a great, intimate, loving purpose, it can be completed. It can be finished in the sense in which a novel can be finished – not because the writer got fed up of the trials of writing, but because they have, through plenty of difficulties, brought the project to a good resolution. Or – more poignantly, perhaps – a relationship can be finished in the way that childhood can be finished. Thanks to the devotion of their parents, a child arrives at the point at which, in order to progress further, they need to leave home. They are not being kicked out in anger or running away in despair; they are leaving because the work of childhood has been done. This is not a rejection of love; it is love's good consequence. Finishing is not a sign of failure, but of background success.

The difference in these cases is that we have clearly understood what all our efforts were for. There was a goal in mind: the writing should not go on forever; the child should leave home. But because we have not asked what our relationship is for, we can't normally achieve this sense of having reached a proper ending. Or else we are refusing to ask because the only motive for the relationship is to ensure that we are not alone – which is never a good enough reason to monopolise someone else's life.

In an ideal relationship, the sense of completion would be mutual. The painful reality, however, is that we may sometimes want to leave while our partner wants us to stay together. But the idea of love as education can still apply: our unbearable conflicts mean that we have stopped being able to teach one another any thing. We may know important qualities they should learn, but we're not the right teacher; we currently lack the patience, skill, charm or self-confidence to transmit insights in a way that will work for them. We have done all we can. Our task is complete not because our partner has nothing left to learn, but because we aren't the right person to guide them; we are entitled to leave without feeling we are abandoning anyone. We can avoid feeling devastated by a break-up by knowing that there are still many other ways in which we need to develop. We may have learnt so much, but we are still far from complete. It is just that the lessons we now have to take on board are going to come from someone else – or from the always educative experience of being on our own for a while.

The hardest person in the world to break up with

Break-ups are almost invariably difficult, but there may be different degrees of complexity at stake in different situations. There exists a cataclysmically painful but little-known type who we might describe as the hardest person in the world to break up with.

A relationship with this type begins like this: you are very drawn to them. Perhaps you are attracted to them physically, and their personality is compelling as well. You admire them and, in areas, feel sympathy for them too; there is probably something in their past that really interests and touches you. You have no desire to break up; in fact, you'd love this to last till the end.

For their part, they seem to be keen on you. They show no interest in leaving you. They want this to be for the long term; perhaps forever.

There is a problem, however, so grave yet so hidden, so damaging yet so hard to grasp, that you can only face up to it slowly. You realise that the partner whom you love and who says they love you is having a grievously detrimental effect on your mental or physical well-being.

What wrong might the partner be perpetrating? It is a spectrum. At one extreme, they might be physically abusive. But the spectrum is long and contains all sorts of insidious ways in which, without ever raising a hand, one human can badly damage another. They might be having affairs, or spending too much money. They might be addicted to something. Or – and this can be hard to get a grip on – they may be constantly 'absent'. They show no reliable warmth towards you; they never initiate any touch; they may never hug. They are present but not really there.

Probably, as soon as these problems first arose, you started to complain. But you did so softly, or sarcastically, or bitterly. Not head-on. After all, you love them and you're a good boy or girl. It can take a long time – years, decades – before you find your voice and feel able to raise an adult objection. What then happens when you ask these types to face up to the harm they are doing to you? There are two main responses.

1. They confess it

Fed up at last, you tell them that you've had enough of the violence, affairs, addiction, over-spending, distance, lack of intimacy, lack of sex ... Instead you proffer an ultimatum. If they don't raise their game, you will leave (even though of course that's the last thing you really want; you love this person!).

You may be shaking and flushed after you have spoken. You're feeling you might be crazy (surely it's crazy to threaten to leave someone you love and who says they love you). You had expected all sorts of dark responses on their part. But something that appears lovely now happens. They admit it! They confess! They say, 'My goodness you're right! I hadn't really fully realised until now, until you finally opened my eyes to how I've harmed you. Baby, I hear you! Baby, I'm so sorry!'

The person promises that they will change. They just need a little bit of time; they need your understanding. They suggest getting a therapist, once a month or so, to get on top of their issues. Their ready candour is moving and suggests they have a handle on their psyches. You are, in any case, desperate to believe them, so they have a willing audience.

The problem is that, despite their promises, the person doesn't change. They make a short-term adjustment, enough to ensure you won't leave them in the timescale you were threatening, but not profound enough to correct the problem – or allow you your freedom.

In the gap between their promise to change and your realisation that they don't have the ability (or perhaps intention) to do so, children may have been born (they wanted kids to keep you around; you wanted them as a token of the happy future that was being promised). Commitments pile up and there are fewer options left in the world beyond. You might not be so young any more.

2. They deny it

However hideous all the above sounds, there is an even worse kind of relationship to leave than that. This is one with the same dynamics, but with one extra twist. When you finally confront them with the problem, they don't confess; they deny it. They tell you you're dreaming. You're imagining it; the problem lies with you, they say. At the same time, they become incensed and offended at the suggestion you're making. 'You're so cynical about me. Don't you trust me?! How rude you are about me! Why don't you have more faith in me and in us?' And they push back: 'you're just as neurotic as you say I am. The problem is with you and not me ...'

This is minefield territory. Relationships and their interactions are generally not filmed, so it's hard for you to back up your claims or even be sure of your verdicts when they are relentlessly challenged. Is the loved one spending too much money, or am I just nagging? Are they actually flirting, or am I just jealous? Are they failing to initiate sex, or am I just insecure?

The partner whom you love and really don't want to leave, and who says they love you, adds to the difficulty by telling you, with authority, that you're crazy; that you're seeing things; that you're too demanding; that there's something wrong with you ...

You are probably an open-minded, nice, intelligent person – and open-minded, nice, intelligent people tend to give others the benefit of the doubt. After all, such types know they aren't perfect. They're aware of everything they get wrong; they don't feel they are brilliant in every way. Perhaps it's plausible that here, too, you may be seeing things that aren't really there. Why insist, especially when you love your partner and want to be with them? Here is a nice person telling you that you're a bit mad and imagining things. It's a dispiriting message, but if disregarding your impulses (and your emotional needs) is the price you pay for keeping a relationship aloft, maybe it's worth thinking of yourself as a bit insane. At least you'll still have a partner.

So, more time passes, and you stay put. In that time, probably there are more children, more entanglements and less of life left for you to build on afterwards. There is also likely to be a destruction of your sense of reality. You will probably start to feel as mad as you're being subtly told you are. You might have a breakdown – which isn't an ideal backdrop against which to leave anyone.

All that said, in both of the above cases, you will have to leave eventually. Your long-term mental well-being depends on it. You will feel extremely alone with this decision. You will be left to wrestle either with feelings that you are nasty (for leaving someone who promises again and again to change) or that you are mad (for leaving someone who tells you that you're demented to doubt their sincerity). You will have to destroy a relationship on the basis of an inner sense that your partner is doing something detrimental to your well-being and cannot stop themselves from doing it, despite telling you they love you.

In order to leave, you will need to think: 'I am in love with someone who is damaged. They cannot realistically change and may even be using me as a reason not to change. Or they are in denial and are abusing my credulity and self-doubt not to look more honestly into themselves.' You will have to think: 'there is probably something in my past, a history of putting up with intolerable situations, that makes me a long-term sucker for this sort of suffering.'

Mountain climbers know that certain peaks cannot be climbed alone; you need a climbing buddy. In this context, let's call them a psychotherapist or a very good friend – the sort who can reassure you of your sanity and who can be there for you when you feel as if you're making the worst choice in the world, even though you are making the very best decision of your life.

Beyond masochism

One of the more surprising and yet effective things we might learn about ourselves is that we are, and perhaps always have been, masochists – an idea as confronting as it can be helpful and revelatory. The word derives (somewhat unfairly for him and his family) from the 19th-century Austrian aristocrat and writer Leopold von Sacher-Masoch (1836–1895).

As a young man, Leopold made a conventional marriage to a fellow member of the nobility, Aurora von Rümelin, but he discovered that his sexual tastes could not be accommodated within the relationship. When he was contacted by an admiring reader, Baroness Fanny Pistor, ostensibly seeking help with her writing, he was able to discover a new aspect to his sexual identity. What he wanted was for Fanny to dress in a fur coat, flog him, dominate him and treat him with haughty cruelty. He wanted Fanny to call him 'Gregor' (a popular servant's name at that time) and, when they travelled, despite being far wealthier than her, he insisted on being forced to sit in third class while she took her place in first.

Leopold's proclivities, which he wrote up in a lightly disguised novella called *Venus in Furs*, caught the interest of the Austrian psychiatrist Richard von Krafft-Ebing (1840–1902). Despite protestations from Leopold's family, he included them in his landmark compendium of kinks, *Psychopathology of Sex* (1890), thereby introducing the world to the term 'masochist': a person sexually aroused by receiving pain.

We now understand a sexual masochist as somebody who might want to be called obscenities, have their hair pulled or their skin scratched, or be ordered to describe themselves in derogatory and humiliating terms (with consent, it must be stressed; anything else would merely be abusive). The mystery is why this could prove so appealing, to which psychotherapy has an answer. For the masochist, cruel treatment in sex play is experienced as relief from the inauthenticity and alienating sentimentality that can otherwise flow from being treated with generous respect. At a deep and compartmentalised level masochists tend not to think too highly of themselves. They harbour intense suspicions of their own characters and nature, believing themselves to be at least in part wicked and impure, and therefore unworthy of unconflicted gentleness and good manners. If others insist on handling them with kid gloves, they cannot feel seen and understood. It only starts to seem properly real and hence properly exciting when a special partner spots the very deep secret about them: that they are (at least for a time and in a certain way) a little shit who deserves a severe beating.

Although the phenomenon of masochism began with and has remained most fully connected to sex, it exists no less powerfully in the emotional realm. Indeed, there may be many more emotional masochists at large than there are sexual ones – and certainly many more of us who are unaware of our own proclivities in this area.

As with sexual masochism, emotional masochism is rooted in self-suspicion. Emotional masochists do not deep down feel as if they are loveable people worthy of careful appreciation and kindness. A powerful aspect of them suspects that they might be stupid pieces of shit. If someone were to enter their orbit and tell them otherwise, if they were to revere and praise them, flatter and stroke them, the emotional masochist might choke on an instinctive sense of disgust at a suitor who seemed not to understand the truth about them, and would soon dismiss them as needy and deluded. Why would anyone feel better about them than they feel about themselves? The emotional masochist will instead direct their energies towards relationships with people whose behaviour will accord much more tightly and reassuringly with their own self-assessments: those who can be guaranteed to act sarcastically, unfaithfully or frigidly.

It is an innocent enough error to fall into a relationship with an unsatisfactory person – the healthiest among us do so all the time. What marks out the masochist is their inability to exit a grim union. They can't imagine life without the person who makes life intolerable.

In the end, the difference between sexual and emotional masochists is that the former tend to know that this is what they are. In order to stop being an emotional masochist, it is vital to start to imagine that one might be an emotional masochist; to see – perhaps for the first time – the ways in which one is engaged in self-sabotage and has made an unconscious commitment to loneliness and frustration. The task is also to see that the origins of all this lie, as ever, in early life. The masochist is liable to have relied on the affections of a parental figure who exhibited, alongside love, a high degree of cruelty, neglect or violence, leading the child to a conviction that their destiny lies in suffering rather than fulfilment.

The most relevant difference between sexual and emotional masochism is that the former will, in the right circumstances, be a lot of fun, whereas the latter is only ever bitter hell. We owe it to ourselves to see the myriad ways in which we may have been holding ourselves back, not out of any kink or necessity, but because our past has unfairly imbued us with a sense that a terrible life is all we deserve.

Why, once you understand love, you can love anyone

Irrespective of whether you consider Jesus to be a popular itinerant preacher or the son of God, there is something very unusual about his views on love. He not only spoke a great deal about love, but also advocated that we love some surprising people.

At one point (described in chapter 7 of Luke's Gospel), he goes to a dinner party and a local prostitute turns up, much to the disgust of the hosts. But Jesus is friendly and kind and defends her against everyone else's criticism. In a way that shocks the other guests, he insists that she is a good person at heart.

In another story (in Matthew, chapter 8), Jesus is approached by a man affected with leprosy. He's in a terrible state. But Jesus isn't shocked and does not shy away from him; instead he reaches out his hand and touches the man. Despite the man's horrendous appearance, here is someone (in Jesus's eyes) that is deserving of closeness and kindness. In a similar vein, at other times, Jesus argues that tax collectors, thieves and adulterers are not to be thought of as outside the circle of love.

Many centuries after Jesus's death, the medieval thinker Thomas Aquinas (1225–1274) defined what Jesus was getting at in this way of talking about love: the person who truly understands love could love anyone. In other words, true love is not specific in its target; it doesn't fixate on particular qualities; it is open to all of humanity, even (and in a way especially) its less appealing examples.

Today this can sound like a strange notion of what love is, because our background ideas about love tend to be closely tied to a dramatic experience: that of falling in love; that is, finding one very specific person immensely attractive, exciting and free of any failings or drawbacks. Love is, we feel, a response to the overt perfection of another person.

However – via some admittedly extreme examples – a very important aspect of love is pushed to the fore in Jesus's vision – and we don't have to be a Christian to benefit from it.

At the heart of this kind of love is an effort to see beyond the outwardly unappealing surface of another human, in search of the tender, interesting, scared and vulnerable person inside.

What we know as the 'work' of love is the emotional, imaginative labour that is required to peer behind an off-putting facade. Our minds tend to resist such a move. They follow well-worn grooves that feel at once familiar and justified. For instance, if someone has hurt us, we naturally see them as horrible. The thought that they might themselves be hurting inside feels weird. If a person looks odd, we find it difficult to recognise that there might be many touching things about them deep down.

If unpleasant events happen in someone's life – if they lose their job, or start drinking too much, or even develop a serious illness – we might be tempted to hold them responsible for their misfortunes. It takes quite a deliberate, taxing effort of the mind to move away from these established responses. To do so might mean taking an unappealing-looking person and trying to imagine them as a young child, joyfully playing on their bedroom floor. We might try to picture their mother, not long after their birth, holding them in their arms, overcome by passionate love for this new little life. Or perhaps drunk and passed out, ignoring their desperate cries.

We might see a furious person in a restaurant violently complaining that the tomato sauce is on the wrong place on their plate, but imagine how unequipped they are to understand, let alone patiently explain their own needs to others, and how powerless they must feel in a world that has frustrated them to the core.

The more energy we expend on thinking like this, the more we stand to discover a very surprising truth: that we could potentially see the loveable aspects of pretty much anyone.

That doesn't mean we should give up all criteria when searching for a partner. It's a way of saying that the nicest person will eventually require us to look at them with imagination as we try to negotiate around some of their gravely dispiriting facets.

Of course, the traffic isn't all one way. We too are challenging to be around and therefore in need of a constantly imaginative tender gaze to rescue us from being dismissed as just another everyday monster or leper.

Intimacy and closeness

One of the frequent and painful paradoxes of romantic life is that the more we get to know and love someone, the harder it can be to summon up any wish to sleep with them. Intimacy and closeness, far from fostering deeper sexual desire, can be the ingredients that destroy excitement, whereas having only recently met a person and not feeling too much for them can set up awkward yet compelling preconditions for wanting to take them to bed.

The conundrum is sometimes colloquially referred to as the 'Madonna/whore complex'. It can sound offensive and reactionary phrased like this, as if the problem applied to only one gender and might condone or even promote the dynamic that it describes. Yet the phrase circles some-thing significant, always contemporary and of relevance to every gender (it might, for heterosexual women, be known as the 'saint/brute complex').

Sigmund Freud first drew attention to our difficulties con-necting love with desire in the essay 'On the Universal Tendency to Debasement in the Sphere of Love' (1912). Of many of his patients, he wrote: 'Where they love, they have no desire, and where they desire, they cannot love.'

In seeking to explain the division, Freud pointed to two facts connected to our upbringing: first, in childhood, we are generally brought up by people we love deeply and yet towards whom we cannot express sexual feelings (dissuaded as we are by a strict incest taboo); second, as adults, we tend to choose lovers who in certain powerful (though unconscious) ways resemble those whom we loved most dearly as children.

Together, these influences set up a devilish conundrum whereby the more deeply we come to love someone outside of our family, the more strongly we are reminded of the intimacy of our early familial bonds, and hence the less free we instinctively are to express our sexual desires without fear or reservation. An incest taboo originally designed to limit the genetic dangers of inbreeding can thus inhibit and eventually ruin our chances of enjoying intercourse with someone to whom we are not related.

The likelihood of the incest taboo's re-emergence with a partner increases greatly after the arrival of children. Until then, reminders of the parental prototypes on which our choice of lovers is subconsciously based can just about be kept at bay. But once there is a pram in the hallway and a sweet infant referring to the person we once tied up or explored with a sex toy as 'Mummy' or 'Daddy', both parties may start to take fright, complain of feeling tired and turn in early.

A dichotomy grows between the 'pure' things one can do with a partner one loves and the 'dirty' things one still longs to do but can only imagine being free enough to do with a near stranger. It can feel untenably disrespectful to want to make love to or (to put the matter at its sharpest) fuck the kind person who will later be preparing lunch boxes and arranging the school rota.

To overcome the problem, it pays to observe that not all childhoods are equal in their tendencies to generate sexual difficulties for people in later life. A parent who is uncomfortable with their body may send out covert signals that sex is dirty, bad and dangerous, and thereby give their child the impression that sex can't belong within a loving relationship. A more integrated and mature parent, on the other hand, may suggest that they are reconciled to their desires and relaxed about some of the proto-sexual things that small children naturally and innocently do: make a lot of noise and mess, take an interest in their bodies and (at a certain age) talk endlessly about poo.

A lot of the work to repair the love/sex dichotomy can, strangely for something so physical, be done in the mind.

We can conceptually start to rehabilitate sex as a serious and, in its way, respectable topic in which good people who love their children and their jobs and are invested in an upstanding life can be profoundly interested; that there need be no conflict between a longing to be filthy and depraved at some points and decorous and respectable at others. We can contain multitudes: the person who wants to flog or be debased and the person who wants to advise, nurture and counsel. One can be whore and Madonna, brute and saint. Rather than seeking out different partners, we might settle, less disruptively, on merely adopting different roles.

A child cannot express love and sexuality to a parent, and vice versa. But it is one of the privileges of adulthood that we no longer have to be hampered by such paradigms. Our lovers need not be only cosy co-parents and responsible, sweet friends; they can also be something else that is important to our well-being and the survival of our relationships: partners in crime.

Accepting ourselves sexually

Theoretically, we live in sexually liberated times. Officially, modern societies have become open-minded about what consenting adults get up to in private. However, this has not removed the likelihood of being beset by profound feelings of shame. As individuals, we tend to remain grievously constrained about what we can admit to liking or wanting in bed. It is hard not to consider our true sexual appetites with embarrassment, and to be either very restricted or outright mute with our partners about who we really are in sexual terms. Rather than sex being the exciting, playful adventure we might have imagined, it often ends up a minefield of disappointment, compromise and caution.

Ironically, the main obstacle to accepting and then explaining the more complicated parts of our sexual nature to other people is that we don't have a reasonable or kindly view of it ourselves. We fear that others will find us weird or confusing because, secretly, that's how we appear to ourselves.

The sense that we need to hide, deny and bury away key elements of who we are is not good for us. When we repress things that are important, they make themselves heard in other ways. As psychoanalysis has revealed, the 'dirty' parts of ourselves can show up disguised as greed, harsh opinions, bad temper, the longing to boss other people about, alcoholism or other forms of risky, damaging behaviour. There is a high price for disavowing powerful parts of ourselves.

The core skill for a more properly liberated sexuality is a richer, more enlightened vision of what sexual desire actually aims at. It is easy to become disgusted with ourselves because our desires seem so opposed to our more caring or intelligent sides. But properly understood, the most apparently 'dirty' or peculiar practices reveal a logic that is far more connected than we might have imagined to our standard self-image and sense of dignity.

For example, if we want to be aggressive and forceful in sex and maybe handcuff a lover or whip them hard, we have not taken leave of our senses. This can be an exciting prospect because it carries with it the promise that our aggression may not always be destructive. It can be allied to an underlying feeling of love, and therefore suggests that we can unite our powerful and our tender sides in a single act. The fantasy is that someone else will acknowledge our strength and wisdom, will recognise our talents and will put us wholly in charge of them. No more need for restraint; no more need to hold our tongue. In the sexual fantasy, someone puts themselves in our hands, as we always hoped might happen. This is an attempt to address the very delicate and very real problem of when one is right to exercise decisive power over another person. In the sexual game, instead of this being a situation fraught with anxiety – because one might be mistaken about another's wishes, because there might be resentment, because one might hurt someone – the commands are met only with delight by the person on whom they are exercised.

Or suppose we want to be humiliated and shouted at in a sexual scenario. We may be turned on by the idea of passivity and submission as a form of escape from the over-strenuous demands of grown-up life. Being a 'slave' means that someone else will know exactly what you should do, will take full responsibility, will take choice away from you. This can sound appalling because most slave owners we can imagine (or even just most bosses) are awful. They won't have our best interests at heart. They won't be kind. So we want to be independent in part because there doesn't seem to be anyone around nice enough to deserve our submission. But the deep hope in the erotic scenario is that at last we can be with someone who is worthy of our complete loyalty and devotion.

The essence
of sexual
liberation
should
be mental.

It is a common feature of all sexual fantasies that they do not – of course – genuinely solve the problems from which they draw their excitement. But we shouldn't worry if the fantasy fails to solve the problem in reality. What we're looking for is simply a way of explaining and sympathising with a desire.

Our sexual imagination can seem frightening at times when it advances scenarios that would be problematic in reality. But we already know how to juggle fantasy in other areas of our lives. For instance, we might enjoy reading a novel in which the central character is interrogated by the secret police; it's a thrilling episode in the book, although it would be traumatic to undergo such an ordeal in real life. The fact that we enjoy a chapter says little about our views on reality.

Sexual excitement is fairly easy to understand and not contrary to reason. It is continuous with many of the things we want in other areas. Although our erotic enthusiasms might sometimes sound odd or off-putting, they are motivated by a search for the good; a search for a life marked by understanding, sympathy, trust, unity, generosity and kindness. The things that turn us on are almost always solutions to things we fear and symbols of how we'd like things to be. The essence of sexual liberation should be mental: in our own heads we can properly articulate the legitimacy and sanity of our interests and excitements. And if we can first explain something calmly and clearly to ourselves, we have a much greater chance of being able subsequently to explain it to a lover.

The experience of erotic liberation does not depend on being able to locate a special person who understands us; it's to do with feeling that we can offer a proper explanation of ourselves to other people. They might or might not be interested in the things that interest us, but we're freed from caring so much about their approval because we already have approval from a source that matters much more: ourselves.

An attractive mindset

Our societies pay vast attention to the idea of 'sexiness'. Far more questionably, they tempt us to believe that it might be easy to understand what this quality consists of. The leading suggestion takes its starting point from the biological sciences: we learn that sex aims at successful reproduction and genetic fitness in the coming generation. Therefore, 'sexiness' must logically comprise a host of semi-conscious signals of fertility and of resistance to disease: bilateral facial symmetry; large, bright pupils; full lips; youthful skin and thick hair.

But this analysis too quickly assumes that it might be simple to know what sex really aims at. Unlike most other living beings, our biological drives sit alongside, and at points take second place to, a range of emotional priorities. Chief among these is the desire to overcome loneliness and share our vulnerability within the arms of a safe and intimate other. We seek, through a physical act, to overcome our customary psychological alienation and a host of painful barriers to being known and accepted. Viewed through such a lens, the erotic is not so much a promise of reproductive health as a suggestion of a redemptive capacity for closeness, connection and understanding, and an end to shame and isolation.

It is this emotional mission that explains the conundrum sometimes generated by people whom one would expect, by standard biological criteria, to possess an exemplary sexual aura, but who leave us cold – just as it may shed light on the associated puzzle of those physically more challenged candidates who nevertheless have a rare power that far outstrips the quality of their hair or the lustre of their eyes.

The people whom we call 'sexy' despite, or aside from, the raw facts of their appearance are those whose features and manner suggest an unusual ability to fulfil the underlying emotional purpose of lovemaking. The way they respond to a joke, the curve of an eyebrow, the characteristic motion of their forehead, the way of holding their hands all convey that one is in the presence of a kindly being who may understand our broken and confused aspects. They may help us over our loneliness and submerged sadness and reassure us of our basic legitimacy and worth; they are someone with whom we can reduce our normal suspicions, cast aside our armour and feel safe, playful and accepted. Whatever the quality of their skin or balance of their proportions, it is these aspects that have a true power to excite us; in a melancholy and avoidant world, this is the real turn-on.

We hear so much about what we might need to do to increase our physical appeal. But by getting more detailed about the psychological traits that drive desire, we could learn to pay as much, if not more, attention to the foundations of an exciting mindset. Armed with a broader understanding of the aims of sexuality, some of the following might also deserve to be counted as valuable sources of sexiness.

A sense of being at odds with mainstream society

Whether at work, with friends or around family, we are often hemmed in by exhausting requirements to fit in and subscribe to dominant notions of what it means to be good and acceptable. These requirements leave behind, or censor, a lot of our internal reality; there ends up being a lot we must not say and even more that we should not even feel. What a relief then to note (perhaps via a wry twitch in another's upper lip) that we are in the presence of someone who knows how to adopt a gently sceptical perspective on prevailing assumptions – someone with whom we would be able to break away and express doubts about revered ideas or people and cast a cathartically caustic gaze on the normal rules of life. Good sex promises to feel like something of a conspiracy against everyone else.

The more we are honest with and exploratory about ourselves, the more we realise that there is much inside our characters that might surprise or horrify outsiders; that we possess alarming degrees of vulnerability, meanness, strangeness, waywardness and folly. Our standard response may be shame and embarrassment, yet we quietly hunger to be properly witnessed and accepted as we really are. What may prove supremely sexy, therefore, are suggestions that another person has explored their own deeper selves with courage, has a handle on their darkness and may, on this basis, be capable of extending an uncensorious perspective on our own.

A tension between 'good' and 'bad'

Someone who paid no attention whatsoever to decency and scoffed at all propriety might be merely alarming. Yet what can prove uniquely appealing is a person alive both to duty and temptation, to the pull of maturity and the draw – at least for a little while, in the early hours – of wickedness; a divided person simultaneously responsible and marked by a touch of desperation.

Vigour and impatience

In addition to this might come a potential for aggression and anger that they manage to keep under control in daily life, but that they know how to release in private; someone whose capacity for a little cruelty is all the more moving because it stands out against a customary habit of consideration and gentleness.

Kindness

A lot of our reality deserves compassion and sympathy. How compelling, therefore, to come across someone whose features might belie a willingness to extend charity towards a lot that is less than perfect in human nature; someone who could know how much we need forgiveness, and who could laugh generously with and at us – because they know how to do the same in relation to themselves.

We have allowed our concern for sexiness to be coarsened by physical obsession because we are under the sway of an overly simplistic biological sense of what sex might be aiming at. Yet by recovering contact with some of what we emotionally crave from another person, we can rediscover that the real turn-on is never just a well-polished body but, always and primordially, a well-fashioned soul.

4

Work

You could finally leave school

Technically, most of us leave school at 16 or 18 – an event that tends to be vividly etched in our memory and surrounded by considerable ceremony and emotion. Yet, despite appearances, many of us don't manage to leave school at that point at all. In a deep part of our minds, we may still be there, deep into adulthood, not sitting in a classroom precisely, but in terms of how our minds work, as much stuck within the confines of a school-based worldview as if we were showing up for assembly every day. This generates immense and unnecessary degrees of unhappiness and compromise for ourselves.

These are some hallmarks of an enduring school-like way of thinking:

- A belief that those in authority know what they are doing and that one's task is to jump through the hoops they set for us. There is a desire to please teachers and win prizes, cups and ribbons.

- A sense that there is an implicit curriculum out there – an externally mandated map of what one needs to do to succeed – and that a wise person must dutifully subscribe to its demands.

- A feeling that when it's going well, work should feel irksome, dull and somewhat pointless. Schools teach us to forget, or ignore, the clues offered to us by our own boredom. They teach us dangerous degrees of patience. They subtly train us in intellectual masochism.

- You're doing it for someone else; an audience; your teachers, your parents and their substitutes in adult life. Make us proud. You have to shine. We've given you so much. What matters is the performance, not any inner sense of satisfaction.

- Authority is benign. They want what is good for you and they speak on behalf of your long-term interests. Don't think you could ever know better; distrust your instincts. We'll look after you. If you follow our rules, you will thrive.

- The exam (and all its successors) are fundamentally accurate. Those who know have worked out the ultimate test of your value. You are what you score.

- Every school is a miniature society, equipped with a strong sense of what values to revere and codes to follow. Bullies lurk, ready to mock and identify any departures from the norm. You can't escape them; they are next to you in class every day. They will spot and persecute the weirdos; they can ruin your life. You learn to cower and adjust your attitudes. Following the herd is paramount.

These ways of thinking don't require us to be sitting in a geography class. We might be in an office selling garden furniture to the Belgian market and thinking like this; we might have children of our own and by all appearances be an adult, yet still be living as though there were 'exams' to pass and cups to be won.

What would it mean to break the mould? What would it mean finally to leave school? It would involve knowing some of the following:

- There is no one way, no one set path to fulfilment laid out by authority figures. 'They' don't know. No one knows.

- The safe path may be dangerous to our flourishing.

- Our boredom is a vital tool. It tells us what is slowly killing us, and reminds us that time is monstrously short.

- Authority is not by definition benign. The teachers and their substitutes have no real plan for you except in so far as it suits their own advancement. It might look as if they want your supreme good, but in reality they want you to play their game for their own benefit. At the end, they have no proper prize to offer you. They will give you a colourful card and send you to the golf course and the grave and you will have wasted your life.

- It doesn't matter what the bullies think. No one is normal. You can dare to make enemies; indeed, you must do so as the price to pay for having developed a character and found something to believe in.

We should not be tough on ourselves for lingering so long. School is an immensely impressive system. We start there when we are not much bigger than a chair. For more than a decade, it is all we know. It is the outside world, and those who love us most tell us we should respect it. It speaks with immense authority not just about itself, but about life in general. It is sold to us as a preparation for the whole of existence. But the main thing it does is to prepare us for yet more school; it is an education in how to thrive within its own profoundly peculiar rules, with only a tenuous connection to the world beyond.

Knowing all this, we might finally work up the courage to leave our inner school – be it at 28, 45 or 62 – and enter the wider, boundless world we have been in flight from for too long.

Overcoming the
pressure to be exceptional

It's a simple question that gets to the core of someone's sense of well-being and legitimacy: did your childhood leave you feeling that you were, on balance, OK as you were, or did you derive the impression that you needed to be extraordinary in order to deserve a place on Earth? To raise an associated question: are you now relaxed about your status, or else a manic overachiever – or filled with shame at your so-called mediocrity?

Around one-fifth of us will be in the uncomfortable cohort, alternately refusing to believe that anything could ever be enough or cursing ourselves as 'failures' (by which we in essence mean that we have not managed to beat insane statistical odds). At school, we probably worked very hard, not because we were drawn to the topics, but because we felt compelled for reasons that were not clear at the time; we just knew we had to come close to the top of the class and revise every evening. We may not be exceptional right now, but we are seldom without an acute sense of pressure to be so.

In childhood, the story might have gone like this. A parent needed us to be special – by virtue of intelligence, looks or popularity – in order to shore up a floundering sense of their own self. The child needed to achieve and could not, therefore, just be; their own motives and tastes were not to be part of the picture. The parent was privately in pain, unable to value themselves, battling an unnamed depression, furious with the course of their own lives, perhaps covertly tortured by their spouse. The child's mission, for which there was no option but to volunteer, was to make it all better.

It seems odd to look at achievement through this lens – not as the thing the newspapers tell us it is, but very often as a species of mental illness. Those who put up the skyscrapers, write the bestselling books, perform on stage or make partner may in fact be the unwell ones. Conversely, the characters who, without agony, can bear an ordinary life, the so-called contented 'mediocrities', may be the emotional superstars, the aristocrats of the spirit, the captains of the heart. The world divides into the privileged who can be ordinary and the damned who are compelled to be remarkable.

The best possible outcome for the latter is to have a breakdown. Suddenly, after years of achievement, they can – if they are lucky – no longer get out of bed. They fall into a profound depression. They develop all-consuming social anxiety. They refuse to eat. They babble incoherently. They in some way poke a very large stick in the wheels of day-to-day life and are allowed to stay home for a while. A breakdown is not merely a random piece of madness or malfunction, it can be a very real – albeit inarticulate and inconvenient – bid for health. It is an attempt by one part of our minds to force the other into a process of growth, self-understanding and self-development that it has hitherto been too cowed to undertake. If we can put it paradoxically, it is an attempt to jump-start a process of getting well – properly well – through a stage of falling very ill.

In an apparently ill state, we might cleverly be seeking to destroy all the building blocks of our previous driven yet unhappy careers. We may be trying to reduce our commitments and our outgoings. We may be trying to throw off the cruelty of others' expectations.

Our societies – which are often unwell at a collective and not just an individual level – are predictably lacking in inspiring images of good-enough ordinary lives. They tend to associate these with being a loser. We imagine that a quiet life is something that only a failed person without options would ever seek. We relentlessly identify goodness with being at the centre, in the metropolis, on the stage. We don't like autumn mellowness or the peace that comes once we are past the meridian of our hopes. But there is, of course, no centre; or rather, the centre is oneself.

Occasionally an artist will bring such bathetic wisdom home. Here is the French writer and philosopher Michel de Montaigne (1533–1592), capturing the point in the third volume of his *Essays*, written a few years before his death:

> 'Storming a breach, conducting an embassy, ruling a nation are glittering deeds. Rebuking, laughing, buying, selling, loving, hating and living together gently and justly with your household – and with yourself – not getting slack nor belying yourself, is something more remarkable, more rare and more difficult. Whatever people may say, such secluded lives sustain in that way duties which are at least as hard and as tense as those of other lives.'

In the late 1650s, the Dutch artist Johannes Vermeer (1632–1675) painted a picture called *The Little Street* which continues to challenge our value system to this day.

Johannes Vermeer, *The Little Street*, c. 1657–1658

Success might in fact be nothing more than a quiet afternoon with the children, at home, in a modest street. A similar point is made in certain stories by Chekhov or Raymond Carver; in Bob Dylan's *Time Out of Mind*; in the films of Eric Rohmer, in particular *Le Rayon Vert* (1982); and in Thomas Jones's study of *A Wall in Naples* (1782).

Thomas Jones, *A Wall in Naples*, c. 1782

Most movies, adverts, songs and articles, however, do not tend to go this way. They continually explain to us the appeal of sports cars, tropical islands, fame, an exalted destiny, first-class air travel and being very busy. The attractions are sometimes perfectly real, but the cumulative effect is to instil in us the idea that our own lives must be close to worthless.

However, there may be immense skill, joy and nobility involved in what we are up to: in bringing up a child to be fairly independent and balanced; in maintaining a good-enough relationship with a partner over many years despite areas of extreme difficulty; in keeping a home in reasonable order; in getting a lot of early nights; in doing a not very exciting or well-paid job responsibly and cheerfully; in listening properly to other people; and, in general, in not succumbing to madness or rage at the paradox and compromises involved in being alive.

There is already a treasury to appreciate in our circumstances when we learn to see these without prejudice or self-hatred. As we may discover once we are beyond others' expectations, life's true luxuries might comprise nothing more or less than simplicity, quiet friendship based on vulnerability, creativity without an audience, love without too much hope or despair, hot baths and dried fruits, walnuts and the odd sliver of very dark chocolate.

The hard work of laziness

At times, perhaps without knowing why, we slip into a resolutely 'lazy' mood. We're simply not able to write anything new or we can't face setting up more meetings. We don't want to clean the fridge or go out to befriend prospective clients. All we have an appetite for, it seems, is to loll on the sofa and maybe dip randomly into a book, wander down to the shops and buy a packet of biscuits, or spend an hour or so soaking in the bath. We might, at an extreme, merely want to sit by the window and stare at the clouds. For a long time.

In such states of mind, we're liable to be stigmatised as 'lazy' by friends or – more painfully – by our own conscience. Laziness feels like a sin against the bustling activity of modernity; it seems to bar us from living successfully or from thinking well of ourselves. But, to consider the matter from another perspective, it might be that the real threat to our happiness and self-development lies not in our failure to be busy, but in the opposite scenario: in our inability to be 'lazy' enough.

Outwardly idling does not have to mean that we are neglecting to be fruitful. It may look to the world as if we are accomplishing nothing, but, below the surface, a lot may be going on that is both important and, in its own way, very arduous. When we are busy with routines and administration, we are focused on the elements that sit at the front of our minds: we are executing plans rather than reflecting on their value and ultimate purpose. But it is to the deeper, less accessible zones of our inner lives that we have to turn in order to understand the foundations of our problems and arrive at decisions and conclusions that can govern our overall path. Yet these only emerge – shyly and tentatively – when we are brave enough to distance ourselves from immediate demands; when we can stare at clouds and do so-called nothing at all.

We need to distinguish between emotional and practical hard work. Someone who looks active, whose diary is filled from morning till night, who is always running to answer messages and meet clients, may appear the opposite of lazy. But, secretly, there may be a lot of avoidance going on beneath the outward frenzy. Busy people evade a different order of undertaking. They are always active, yet don't get round to working out their real feelings about their work. They constantly delay the investigation of their own direction. They are lazy when it comes to understanding particular emotions about a partner or friend. They go to every conference, but don't get around to thinking about what their status means to them.

We need to distinguish between emotional and practical hard work.

They regularly catch up with colleagues, but don't consider what the point of money might be. Their busyness is a subtle but powerful form of distraction.

Our minds are, in general, a great deal readier to execute than to reflect. They can be rendered uncomfortable by so-called large questions: What am I really trying to do? What do I actually enjoy and who am I trying to please? How would I feel if what I'm currently doing comes right? What will I regret in a decade's time? By contrast, the easy bit can be the running around, the never pausing to ask why, the repeatedly ensuring that there isn't a moment to have doubts or feel sad or searching. Busyness can mask a vicious form of laziness.

Our lives might be a lot more balanced if we learnt to reallocate prestige, pulling it away from those with a full diary and towards those wise enough to allow for long afternoons of reflection. We should think that there is courage not just in travelling the world, but also in daring to sit at home with one's thoughts for a while, risking encounters with certain anxiety-inducing or melancholy but also necessary ideas. Without the shield of busyness, we might bump into the realisation that our relationship has reached an impasse, that our work no longer answers to any higher purpose or that we feel furious with a family member who is subtly exploiting our patience. The heroically hard worker isn't necessarily the one in the business lounge of the international airport; it might be the person gazing without expression out of the window and occasionally writing down one or two ideas on a pad of paper.

The point of 'doing nothing' is to clean up our inner lives. There is so much that happens to us every day, so many excitements, regrets, suggestions and emotions that we should, if we are living consciously, spend at least an hour a day processing. Most of us manage a few minutes at best and thereby let the marrow of life escape us. We do so not because we are forgetful or bad, but because our societies protect us from our responsibilities to ourselves through their cult of activity. We are granted every excuse not to undertake the truly difficult labour of leading more conscious, more searching and more intensely felt lives.

The next time we feel lazy, we should imagine that a deep part of us is preparing to give birth to a big thought. As with a pregnancy, there is no point hurrying the process. We need to lie still and let the idea gestate, sure that it may eventually prove its worth. We may need to risk being accused of gross laziness in order one day to put in motion projects and initiatives we can feel proud of.

Learning to listen to your boredom

One of the most striking characteristics of small children is their militant aversion to boredom. With ruthless determination, they embark on one occupation after another, shifting their focus whenever an even marginally more attractive prospect comes into view. An average morning might involve taking out eight board games from the cupboard, then, just as it seemed it might be time for Snakes and Ladders, experimenting with turning the sofa into a ski slope, then trying to pull a toy rabbit's tail off, followed by exploring what happens to the chocolate biscuits when one pounds them with a hammer, before finally tipping up all the kitchen chairs and pretending they are ships engaged in a sea battle.

What we call education is in large measure an attempt to bring order to this chaos; to teach the child to ignore the welter of their own spontaneous enthusiasms and instead to learn to sit with their boredom for a while in the name of getting something substantial done: listening to a lengthy speech about kindness by the head teacher without screaming; enduring a forty-five-minute maths lesson without getting up to dance; resisting the temptation to draw an imaginary world during an introductory French class. Becoming that most prized of things, a 'good child', means mastering the art of suppressing one's own boredom in the name of growing up.

The rationale for this pedagogical move is both solid and noble. There is clearly a great deal to be gained from not running away the moment a new fancy enters one's mind. Yet the problem isn't that we're generally blind to this logic, but that we're far too good at submitting to it. Most of us grow fatefully proficient at bearing our own boredom.

Along the way, we forget that boredom has many important things to teach us. It is, at its best, a confused, inarticulate but genuine signal from a deep part of our minds that something is wrong. We may not know what, but the sensation of being bored frequently contains (especially for otherwise sensible adults) an apprehension of genuine danger. There are boring books that should be tossed aside. There are boring people we should refuse to see. There are boring films we should walk out of. And what should sharpen our courage to do so is an ongoing awareness that the fundamental currency of our lives is time, of which we are in desperately short supply, there being on average no more than 26,000 days or so in an entire existence on the planet.

The American essayist Ralph Waldo Emerson (1803–1882) once remarked: 'In the minds of geniuses, we find – once more – our own neglected thoughts.' This implies that most of us become mediocre not because we have failed to submit ourselves rigorously enough to the world's knowledge, but because we have grown too good at ignoring our inborn ideas and impulses. We have smothered our feelings of excitement and boredom for the sake of obedience to grand authorities and have paid a heavy price for our politeness. The people we call geniuses are, from this perspective, not in possession of any form of esoteric wisdom; they are simply unusually faithful towards aspects of their inner lives. They are those who have managed to hold on to things that the rest of us surrender out of an exaggerated fear of being weird or wilful.

Listening to our boredom has the chance to tug us back to our true concerns. We realise what our tastes in literature really are; what sort of entertainment we actually prefer; what properly enthuses us about other people. Boredom functions as the scalpel with which we can cut off all that is 'dead' and extraneous about our lives. The courage to admit to our boredom allows us, gradually, to develop a personality. Boredom is the inarticulate voice of a fundamental idea: that something has been oversold to us and needs to be discounted.

It is telling that, as they get older, many artists instinctively get better at listening to their boredom, and produce greatly superior work as a result. Critics commonly refer to this as a 'late style', marked by impatience, brevity, courage and intensity. One thinks of Bach's exceptional later choral works, the final short stories of Chekhov or the sublime paper cut-outs of the dying Matisse.

Poignantly, an ageing Picasso, on a tour of a primary school, once remarked: 'It took me four years to paint like Raphael, but a lifetime to paint like a child.' What he meant was that it had taken him decades to shake off a compliant urge to paint 'well' and 'respectably' and to listen more closely to his own sense of fun (a serious business, not to be confused with its lesser sibling, frivolity). Pushed by mortality into a new respect for his own centres of pleasure, Picasso learnt how to overcome every trace of the mannered approach of his youth in order to focus on the joy of decorating a canvas with the loose brushstrokes, exuberance and bold colours well known to those natural artistic masters: five-year-old children.

We don't have to be a towering figure of 20th-century art for the point to apply. All of us need to learn to develop a 'late style', and ideally as early on in our lives as possible. This is a way of being wherein we shake off the dead hand

Pablo Picasso, *Academic Study*, 1895

(Made when he was 14.)

Pablo Picasso, *The Pigeons*, 1957 (Made when he was 76.)

Here is an artist who has remembered to listen to their boredom.

of habit and social fear and relearn to listen to what enter-
tains us (and so we can stand the best chance of properly
pleasing others too).

The results should apply not to works of art in a museum,
but to aspects of our intimate lives: to the way we choose
a career, host a dinner party, go on a holiday, have sex,
tell an anecdote or act around our friends. Here too lie
multiple opportunities to cut to the chase, to say what
really matters and to express what we truly feel and want,
while we yawn politely but defiantly at all that is slowly
killing us.

Listening to our boredom has the chance to tug us back to our true concerns.

5

Pleasure

Getting more serious
about pleasure

When it comes to work, we tend to be strategic and thorough in our approach. We think extensively about where our talents and opportunities lie; we spend years (and a fortune) on training; we devote extraordinary energy (and our most vigorous decades) to progressing up the ladder and we keep a vigilant and jealous eye on the progress of our rivals.

By contrast, our leisure hours promise to be easier. We don't expect there to be much complexity in this section of existence. We want to relax and have fun, and we tend to envisage that the only obstacles to such goals might be time and money. We adopt a welcoming, unsuspicious manner and readily take up others' suggestions without gimlet-eyed scrutiny. Sometimes, without thinking about it too much, we end up in a water park or at an aquarium or hosting a barbecue.

What we may miss for many years is the real price of our negligence. We forget that our lives are so much less than they might be because we insist on being haphazard where we might be devotedly analytical. We stick to being guided by hearsay and muddled instinct when we should harness reason and independent reflection; we are a lot more miserable than we might be because we cannot take our own fun more seriously. And we don't because we are touchingly but ruinously lacking in vigilance about our individuality. We assume that what will work for others will work for us too. It doesn't readily occur to us to take our uniqueness into account.

A corrective to this costly absence of mind comes from an unexpected quarter: the history of art. What we call a great artist is someone who has learnt to take their pleasure seriously. Most young artists don't. They like art, of course, but they don't drill too deeply into what they in particular, as unique beings with a highly individual history, sensory system and temperament, are inclined to like. That is why the chief characteristic of inexperienced artists is derivativeness. Their art reflects what everyone else around them tends to like and make in their particular era and circle. It's the art of people without a capacity to take their own pleasure seriously.

Consider, for example, the career of the Swiss artist Alberto Giacometti (1901–1966). Born in the canton of Graubünden, he attended the Geneva School of Fine Arts, and his early work reflects the dominant influences of the times: the work of the Italian artist Giovanni

Segantini and of the Impressionist school, especially Édouard Manet and Henri Fantin-Latour. One thinks of Giacometti's paintings of the Swiss lakes and the surrounding mountains, or of his portraits of family members, such as his sister Ottilia. There is pleasure here, for sure, but not a pleasure with any deep roots in the personality of the creator.

Alberto Giacometti, *View on the Sils Lake Towards Piz Lizun*, 1920

Alberto Giacometti, *Ottilia*, c. 1920

Then, in his early twenties, Giacometti left Switzerland for Paris. He broke with his family, thought very hard about who he really was and eventually re-emerged as the great artist we know today: the maker of unique, haunting, elongated figures that speak to us of a longing and a loneliness we may never have been able to identify in ourselves so clearly.

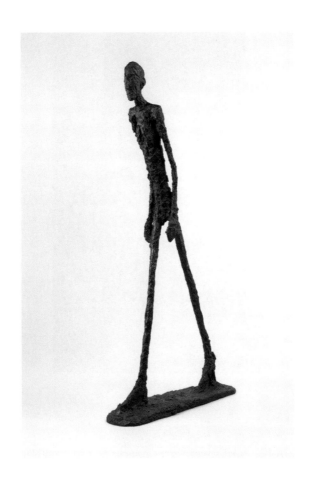

Alberto Giacometti, *Walking Man I*, 1960

To become an artist in this sense is not about technical discovery; it's about the strength to discover and then stay faithful to one's self.

Most of us are not making art. But we are involved in the business of getting to know and please ourselves, as any artist must. For too much of life, we assume that we may be like everyone else. Only gradually, if we are lucky, do we come to see that our characteristic way of drawing pleasure – from nature, books, films, dinner parties, clothes, travels, gardening – bears the imprint and distinctive timbre of our own individuality. To lean on an associated example, we learn how to become proper fetishists. The sexual fetishist is to the ordinary lover like the established artist to the novice: they are someone who has worked out what they really like, and how to hold on to it with rare fidelity and tenacity. While most of us go along with general suggestions of what good sex might consist of, the fetishist discerns their own proclivities. They realise that they might like a particular kind of floral material or a leather watch strap; the sound of water or the feel of a gold chain; a pair of socks or a black monogrammed briefcase. The fetishist is akin to the artist in having the stubborn presence of mind to defend their own tastes, even when these depart from the mainstream.

One thinks in this regard of the modernist architect Le Corbusier's attachment to including ramps in his buildings, whatever the design challenges or his clients' objections, or of a lover who dares to ask their partner to put on a pair of ankle-length white athletic socks before entering the bedroom. Great fetishists, like great artists, know the power of details to generate happiness.

Le Corbusier, Villa Savoye, 1928–1931
The power of details can make us happy.

By contrast, most of us are fatefully modest about what we enjoy. We don't dare to foreground our own discoveries. What we do with our leisure hours is therefore marked by a dispiriting uniformity. We go skiing because we hear so often that it's meant to be fun. We invite guests around for dinner and talk about what everyone else talks about and have melon for a starter because that's what one is meant to do. Our weekends unfold a bit like those of all our colleagues. We die with our particular appetites and intense sensations tragically unexplored.

To save ourselves, we need the equivalent of an artistic breakthrough. We should be prepared to be redemptively weird across the board in our leisure pursuits. If we were to use only ourselves as our lodestar and point of reference, what would a dinner party look like? What would we eat? What would we talk about? Where would we sit? What have we – the 'we' that will be dead in a few decades – enjoyed in the past and what might we recreate going forward? What might a holiday specifically geared to our tastes and proclivities be like? What bit of the standard tourist itinerary might we ditch? Which of our hitherto stray or guilty pleasures might we dare to bring into focus and anchor our days around? What might we learn to say no to and, in contrast, to emphasise going forward?

It is so often drummed into us that we may be selfish and should learn to relinquish our interests for the sake of the community that we fail to notice an even more horrific possibility: that in many areas, we're not selfish enough. We fail to pay appropriate attention to our fragile, extraordinary and scarce natures. We don't give outward expression to our true sensations. We don't give our weekends and our spare time the imprint of our own characters. We kill our uniqueness out of politeness and a fear of being odd. We spend far too much of our brief lives defending an impossible idea: that we are pretty much like anyone else.

A more spontaneous life

One explanation for the low-level sadness that often dogs our spirits is a lack of spontaneity. Without necessarily being aware of the affliction, we can suffer from an excess of orderliness, caution and rigidity; we know pretty much exactly what we'll be doing a year from now; we rarely make a move without having planned it in detail; we seldom go anywhere new on the spur of the moment. Our limbs are tight, our words are measured, our interactions prescribed. Everything is under close surveillance, but not especially satisfying. We haven't danced in a long while.

So what might a more spontaneous life be like? It would be one in which we were able to act with less inhibition and fear in accordance with our true beliefs and values. Around friends, we might, in a rush of unfettered emotion, but without anything romantic being meant by it, tell someone that we love and admire them very much. Or, when upset by someone, we might allow ourselves to communicate hurt and disappointment directly. In company, we could feel free to outline what we actually thought about a political matter hedged in by group-think. In bed, we might share one of our more intense and seldom-mentioned fantasies. In our work, we might embark on a bold and potentially life-changing initiative far sooner than we had imagined. In our leisure time, we might start writing a collection of recipes or poems, or else book a flight at the last minute and end up in a country we have never been to before, on an itinerary that we had made up only that morning.

The opposite of spontaneity is rigidity, an inability to allow too many of our own emotions into consciousness, and a corresponding reliance on hard work, manners and precise timetabling to prevent intimacy with the confusing, intense and unpredictable raw material of life itself. We are rigid because we are afraid. We stay rooted to our familiar spot because any movement is experienced as intensely dangerous. We ruminate excessively as a way of trying to exert control over a chaotic environment through our own thoughts. We seldom act, out of dread of making a terrible mistake.

Spontaneity is almost always something that we have lost, rather than (mysteriously) failed to learn. It is a potential within all of us at birth, but it can be stripped from our characters. If we were to imagine a cruel experiment designed to rid someone of their capacity for spontaneity, one would probably need, at the age of one and a half or so, to frighten them rather a lot (be it over a wish to ruffle an adult's hair, explore a cupboard or sob uncontrollably).

One would have to make the child feel that their emotions were too much to bear or illegal. One would shame them for any signs of exuberance or playfulness. And one might model for them behaviour marked by panic whenever something new appeared on the horizon: an unexpected ring at the door would be a crisis; a holiday a succession of possible catastrophes.

It is in the nature of our psychology that a pattern developed in relation to one particular set of circumstances in childhood becomes a feature of adult character, until and unless we remember and understand its dynamics. In other words, we'll continue not to be spontaneous until we can grasp how and why being so came to feel dangerous. The English psychoanalyst Donald Winnicott spoke of a healthy upbringing being one in which a child was able to express their True Self without too much need, at first, for the compliance and hypocrisy of a False Self. Only when this True Self has had a chance to have its day can a person bear to submit to the demands of the world without too much loss of creativity or initiative. We need – with some urgency – to work out what happened to our True Self.

We should recognise along the way that many of our inhibitions are no longer warranted by the wide-open adult world; that whatever terrors we laboured under as children, we can afford now to relax our muscles, let our limbs hang more loosely from us and take a few risks to express our sexuality, our politics, our enthusiasms and our distastes. We might tell a friend we like them very much indeed; we might get stern with someone who keeps taking advantage of us; we might dare to make a move without a requirement to remove every last vestige of risk. We have for too long been clenched into place as if waiting for a blow that belongs to the past, not the future.

Were we to admire the work of the artist Francis Bacon (1909–1992), it might in part be because it seems to contain a small morality tale about spontaneity. Bacon's canvases were, in their general layout, rigid and coolly formal, made up of sombre colours, symmetrical lines and stark perspectives. But in the middle of this austerity, Bacon typically allowed for a great deal of haphazardness and accident. He introduced figures composed with utmost serendipity, by throwing paint, and sometimes sponges, at the canvas, by pressing his brushes into swirling shapes in a frenzy of calculated disorder.

We might need to do a version of Bacon's experiments in our own lives: to prepare areas of great order and logic, but then allow for moments when we relax the shackles,

Francis Bacon, *Turning Figure*, 1962

safe in the knowledge that not everything is at stake and that the rewards may be decisive. We can throw paint and see how it lands; pay someone a compliment and see what happens; go to another country and be confident of somehow finding a bed for the night; turn our lives a little upside down and trust that they will be interesting at the very least. It may once have felt safe to avoid any risk, but the real risk today is to lead the remainder of our lives without ever giving expression to the spontaneous True Self, hiding inside its cage, terrified and clenched. We can at last (discreetly enough so that no one notices at first) try to dance a little.

Small luxuries

Although it often – and sometimes fairly – gets confused with status seeking and showing off, at its best, luxury represents a concerted effort by one set of humans to provide carefully thought-out pleasure to another. It is, in the material realm, akin to the work of love.

Luxury arises from the attempt to answer the question: if we didn't have to keep costs down, what would be the nicest, kindest and most generous possible version of something – a hotel, villa, car, restaurant or airline seat? Of course, this also means that, most of the time, major luxuries are unaffordable.

But what we too often forget, especially on our sadder, more restricted days, is that the core pleasures of luxury also exist in small forms that can be accessed at a far more manageable cost by pretty much anyone at any time. In certain categories, we can all have the privileges open to monarchs and potentates. We can walk into a fancy bakery and treat ourselves to the very finest brioche roll, wrapped for us with care by a dedicated and proud assistant. We can, when it comes to fruit juice, show maximal decadence and financial heedlessness.

The best way to identify the most suitable micro-luxuries lies in analysing what really appeals to us in the grand ones. For instance, if we think about a fabulous watch, it may turn out that – for us – a central attraction is the beautifully precise engineering of its springs and cogs. Once we have this in mind, we may find that a related and comparable pleasure is available to us when we purchase a high-quality, double-lever corkscrew. At a vastly more modest price point, it too has been superbly designed: its toothed wheels elegantly transform the downward pressure of our hands into an upward thrust; the action is smooth and reassuringly solid. We're accessing the same pleasure zone from an unexpected angle.

Similarly, the world's loveliest cars may be out of our reach, but we could quite easily purchase a box of some of the best pencils in the world. The pencil manufacturers have the same fundamental ambition as the car designers: to take a practical object and make it as pleasurable to use as possible. They have considered what kind of wood is best for sharpening; what surface texture gives the firmest grip; what the ideal weight and balance should be; and what lead gives the most satisfying line. They have aimed at perfection, and the resulting product does not need an exorbitant price tag. We can, on a very modest salary, buy the best pencil available.

The facade of a French chateau on the market for multiple millions may delight us with its refined proportions, but we can buy an equally refined plate and eat a slice of toast off it each morning. One thing that may appeal about a famous hotel is the attentive, discreet service. We can't spend a fortnight in a suite, but we could occasionally have a cocktail in the bar, mixed and served with polite panache.

Luxury exists around all kinds of objects. There are exceptional Old Master paintings, but there is also exceptional olive oil. Someone else might have a bespoke cashmere coat, but we might have a pair of silk socks. In terms of escalating costs, the high point of socks is reached much sooner than the high point in coats. The world's best bread is within our grasp; the world's best caviar may not be.

We misunderstand luxury when we see it as the self-indulgence of the rich or as the stroking of the egos of those who already have inflated views of their own worth. Luxury objects have a power to reassure us and make us feel, for a time, loved and appreciated, and they are often needed precisely because we feel crushed by existence. Luxury can matter because, in other areas of our lives, much has gone wrong, for reasons too complex to correct in any brief timescale. Our child may no longer look up when we greet them at breakfast; our spouse may be filled with resentments; our work may leave us in no doubt as to our idiocy and foolishness.

But, with one loaf of sourdough bread from an artisanal bakery or a tiny bottle of lavender bath oil from a shop in Provence, we have – for a little while – a kind of compensation for our woes. We are in the presence of something truly delightful; a portion of the kindness and consideration we crave, but hardly ever receive and may not quite deserve. Money obviously cannot buy us everything we truly want, especially the warm regard of those we love. But it can put us in contact with a few symbols of consideration and tenderness, which might be the very best we can hope for, and that is realistically available to us, in the radically imperfect circumstances of our lives. We may not always have the inner resources to find luxury uninteresting, but fortunately, in very minor doses, it is continually and surprisingly available to us as a source of consolation and uplift.

Learning to be more selfish

From a young age, we are taught that one of the greatest risks to our integrity and flourishing is our own selfishness. Wherever possible, we must learn to think more of other people, keep in mind how often we fail to see things from their point of view, and be aware of the small and large ways in which we disadvantage and ignore collective interests. Being good means, at its most basic, putting other people more squarely at the centre of our lives.

But for some of us, the problem isn't so much that we are heedless to this advice, but that we take it too much to heart. So mindful are we of the risks of selfishness that we run into an opposite danger: an abnegation of the self; a modesty that borders on self-erasure; a shyness about pressing oneself forward and a manic inability to say 'no' or cause the slightest frustration to others.

As a result of our talent at 'selflessness', we fill our diaries with obligations to people who bore and drain us, we stick at jobs that neglect our true talents and we stay for far too long in relationships with people who deceive us, annoy us or take us for a ride. Then, one morning, we wake up and find that the bulk of our life is already behind us, that our best years are spent and that no one is especially grateful for our sacrifices, that there isn't a reward in heaven for our renunciations and that we are furious with ourselves for mistaking meekness and self-surrender for kindness.

The priority may then be to rediscover our latent reserves of selfishness. The very word may be frightening, because we aren't taught to distinguish between the bad and good versions of this trait. On the one hand, there is the kind of selfishness that viciously exploits and reduces others; that operates with no higher end in view; that disregards people out of meanness and negligence. On the other, there is the kind of selfishness that we require to get anything substantial done; that lends us the courage to prioritise our own concerns over the flotsam and jetsam of daily life; and that lends us the spirit to be more forthright about our interests with people who claim to love us. This type of selfishness can lead us to sidestep nagging demands, not in order to make people suffer, but so that we can husband our resources and, in time, be able to serve the world in the best way we can.

With a more fruitfully selfish philosophy in mind, we might fight to have an hour to ourselves each day. We may do something that could get us labelled as 'self-indulgent' (having psychotherapy three times a week, or writing a book), but that is vital to our spirit. We might go on a trip on our own, because so much has happened that we need to process in silence. We cannot be good to anyone else until we have serviced some of our own inner callings. A lack of selfishness may be the fastest route to turning us into ineffective, embittered and ultimately disagreeable people.

Hindu philosophy can be a useful guide here: it divides our lives into four stages, each with its distinctive roles and responsibilities. The first is that of the bachelor student (known as Brahmacharya); the second that of the householder and parent (Grihastha); and the third that of the grandparent and semi-retired advisor (Vanaprastha). But it's the fourth that is the really interesting age in this context: known as Sannyasa, this is the time when – after years of service to other people, to business, family and society – we finally throw off our worldly obligations and focus instead on the development of our psychological and spiritual sides. We might sell up our house, go travelling and wander the world to learn, talk to strangers, open our eyes and nourish our minds. In the period of Sannyasa, we live simply (perhaps by a beach or on the side of a mountain); we eat basic food and have few belongings; we cut our ties with everyone who has nothing spirit-related to tell us; anyone who is on the make and

and in too much of a hurry; anyone who doesn't spend a substantial amount of their time reflecting on the meaning of being alive.

What feels insightful about this division of existence is that it acknowledges that a Sannyasa way of living can't be right for everyone at any time, yet, on the same score, that no good life can be complete without a version of it. There are years when we simply have to keep our heads down and study; years when we have to bring up children and accumulate some capital. But there are also, just as importantly, years when what we need to do above all is say 'enough' – enough to material and superficial demands; enough to sexual and romantic entanglements; enough to status and sociability – and instead turn our minds inwards and upwards.

Without having to don the orange robe favoured by Hindu Sannyasas, with perhaps few visible signs of our re-orientation to speak of, it is open to all of us to make a psychological move into a more self-focused and inner age. We can convey to those around us that we aren't lazy, mad or callous; we just need to avoid doing the expected things for a while. We need to fulfil our real promise by casting aside an idea that is only ever superficially wise: putting other people first.

We cannot
be good to
anyone else
until we have
serviced some
of our own
inner callings.

6

Freedom

How to lengthen your life

The normal way we set about trying to extend our lives is by striving to add more years to them – maybe by eating more quinoa and broccoli, going to bed early and running in the rain. But this approach may turn out to be quixotic, not only because Death can't reliably be warded off with kale, but at a deeper level, because the best way to lengthen a life is not by attempting to stick more years onto its tail.

One of the most basic facts about time is that, even though we insist on measuring it as if it were an objective unit, it doesn't, in all conditions, feel as if it were moving at the same pace. Five minutes can feel like an hour; ten hours can feel like five minutes. A decade may pass like two years; two years may acquire the weight of half a century.

In other words, our subjective experience of time bears little relation to the way we like to measure it on a clock. Time moves more or less slowly according to the vagaries of the human mind: it may fly or it may drag. It may evaporate into airy nothing or achieve enduring density.

If the goal is to have a *longer* life, whatever the dieticians may urge, it seems like the priority should not be to add raw increments of time, but to ensure that whatever years remain *feel* appropriately substantial. The aim should be to densify time rather than to try to extract one or two more years from the grip of Death.

Why then does time have such different speeds, moving at certain points bewilderingly fast, at others with intricate moderation? The clue is to be found in childhood. The first ten years almost invariably feel longer than any other decade we have on Earth. The teens are a little faster but still crawl. Yet by our 40s, time will have started to trot; by our 60s, it will be unfolding at a bewildering gallop.

The difference in pace is not mysterious; it has to do with novelty. The more our days are filled with new, unpredictable and challenging experiences, the longer they will feel. Conversely, the more one day is exactly like another, the faster it will pass by in a blur. Childhood ends up feeling so long because it is the cauldron of novelty. Its most ordinary days are packed with extraordinary discoveries and sensations: these can be as apparently minor yet as significant as the first time we explore the zip on a cardigan or hold our nose underwater; the first time we look at the sun through the cotton of a beach towel or dig our fingers into the putty holding a window in its frame. Dense as it is with stimuli, the first decade can feel a thousand years long.

Childhood
ends up feeling
so long because
it is the cauldron
of novelty.

By middle age, things can be counted upon to have grown a lot more familiar. We may have flown around the world a few times. We no longer get excited by the idea of eating a pineapple, owning a car or flipping a light switch. We know about relationships, earning money and telling others what to do. As a result, time runs away from us without mercy.

One solution often suggested is that we should put all our efforts into discovering fresh sources of novelty. We need to become explorers and adventurers. We must go to Machu Picchu or Angkor Wat, Astana or Montevideo; we need to find a way to swim with dolphins or order a thirteen-course meal at a world-famous restaurant in downtown Lima. That will finally slow down the cruel gallop of time.

However, this is to labour under an unfair, expensive and ultimately impractical notion of novelty: that it must involve seeing new things when it should really involve seeing familiar things with new eyes. By middle age we may have *seen* a great many things in our neighbourhoods, but we are unlikely to have properly *noticed* most of them. We have probably taken a few cursory glances at the miracles of existence that lie to hand and assumed, quite unjustly, that we know all there is to know about them. We've imagined we understand the city we live in, the people we interact with and, more or less, the point of it all.

Of course, we have barely scratched the surface. We have grown bored of a world we haven't begun to study properly. And that, among other things, is why time is racing by.

The pioneers at making life feel longer in the way that counts are not dieticians, but artists. At its best, art is a tool that reminds us of how little we have fathomed and noticed. It reintroduces us to ordinary things and reopens our eyes to a latent beauty and interest in precisely those areas we had ceased to bother with. It helps us to recover some of the manic sensitivity we had as newborns. Opposite is the French artist Paul Cézanne (1839–1906), looking closely at apples, as if he had never seen one before, and below him is Albrecht Dürer (1471–1528), looking very closely at a clod of earth, as only children usually do.

We don't need to make art in order to learn the most valuable lesson of artists, which is about noticing properly, living with our eyes open – and thereby savouring time. Without any intention to create something that could be put in a gallery, we could, as part of a goal of living more deliberately, take a walk in an unfamiliar part of town;

Paul Cézanne, *Apples*, c. 1878–1879

Albrecht Dürer, *The Great Piece of Turf*, 1503

ask an old friend about a side of their life we'd never dared to probe at; lie on our back in the garden and look up at the stars; or hold our partner in a way we never tried before. It takes a rabid lack of imagination to think we have to go to Machu Picchu to find something new to perceive.

In Fyodor Dostoevsky's novel *The Idiot* (1869), a prisoner has suddenly been condemned to death and been told he has only a few minutes left to live. 'What if I were *not* to die!' he exclaims. 'What if life were given back to me – what infinity! … I'd turn a whole minute into an age …' Faced with losing his life, the poor wretch recognises that every minute could be turned into aeons of time, with sufficient imagination and appreciation.

It is sensible enough to try to live *longer* lives. But we are working with a false notion of what long really means. We might live to be a thousand years old and still complain that it had all rushed by too fast. We should be aiming to lead lives that feel long because we manage to imbue them with the right sort of open-hearted appreciation and unsnobbish receptivity – the kind that five-year-olds know naturally how to bring to bear. We need to pause and look at one another's faces, study the sky, wonder at the eddies and colours of the river and dare to ask the kind of questions that open others' souls. We don't need to add years; we need to densify the time we have left by ensuring that every day is lived consciously. We can do this via a manoeuvre as simple as it is momentous: by starting to *notice* all that we have as yet only *seen*.

A few things to be grateful for

We are geniuses at focusing on what is missing from our lives. Our dissatisfaction generally serves us well; it keeps us from complacency and boredom. But we are also dragged down by a pernicious inability ever reliably to stop, take stock and recognise what isn't imperfect and appalling. In our haste to secure the future, we fail to notice what has not yet failed us, what isn't actually out of reach, what is already very good. We should create small occasions when we pause our striving and, for a few moments, properly take on board some of what we have to be grateful for:

- Most of the 78 organs in our bodies have performed pretty reliably since the day we were born.

- We don't need to be afraid of starving – or even of being very cold.

- Every year, if we just stay in one spot, there are at least two weeks of perfect weather.

- We are never too far from a very hot bath.

- We've sometimes been surprised by how well things turned out.

- We can with complete impunity fantasise about people we can't have.

- We've come a long way since our early shyness, incompetence and fear.

- Everyone messes up their life quite a bit.

- Of course we couldn't have known better.

- Compared with what we feared in the rockiest patches, this is almost OK.

- We're still here.

- There were no outright catastrophes today.

- A few times, we really experienced what love felt like.

- A few times, we really felt understood.

- Many of the people we love are still alive.

- There's always music.

- Without asking anyone, we could go into many shops and buy a treat.

- We could disappear for a bit.

- We're no longer trapped, like children are.

- We still have quite a lot of time left.

- Children of three or four are, intermittently, reliably sweet.

- There hasn't been a war here for a while.

- You can turn on the tap and clean water comes out for almost nothing.

- We can leave the places we were born and raised.

- There's always someone suffering just in the way we are.

- Everyone is weird; we just don't have access to their inner minds.

- The silent majesty of a clear night sky.

- We're very normal in the number of idiocies we've committed.

- We don't have to take ourselves seriously.

- We can feel heroic about an ordinary life.

- We have managed to learn a few things down the years.

- There are lots of beautiful people we can take pleasure in looking at.

- There are people who have loved us, even though we didn't totally deserve their affection or devotion.

- A few bits of our body are rather beautiful.

- Our parents met and managed to make love successfully. And their parents did too. We so nearly didn't even exist.

- People who didn't have to took a serious and benign interest in our education and development.

- Things really do look better when we have slept well.

- Many of the world's most interesting people have written down their thoughts.

- Other people are usually shyer, sweeter and kinder than we'd anticipated.

- We've perhaps found one good friend.

- We can write everything we feel down on paper.

- We can, without too much effort, order a bowl of French fries.

- We once really turned someone else on.

- Others forget the stupid things we've done faster than we do.

- Sincere apologies tend to be gladly accepted.

- We can reinvent ourselves – a bit.

- We didn't turn eighteen in 1939.

- Parents keep on loving us even if we largely ignore them for a few years.

- Children continue to love us even if they say they don't, and even if we were far from perfect parents.

- By the time we are forty, nothing we did or thought at the age of twenty will seem very important.

- No one can stop us having our own thoughts.

- We can get to hear the jokes and stories of the funniest people on the planet.

- In the middle of the night, and in the early morning, we have the world to ourselves.

- It isn't what happened to us that counts, but how we choose to tell the story.

- We do not know what will happen in the future.

Twenty signs of emotional maturity

We are never done with that most precious of goals: becoming a proper grown-up. For this mission, it could help to know what being grown-up might really involve. Here are twenty suggestions:

1. You realise that most of the bad behaviour of other people really comes down to fear and anxiety, rather than (as it is generally easier to presume) nastiness or idiocy. You loosen your hold on self-righteousness and stop thinking of the world as populated by either monsters or fools. It makes things less black and white at first, but, in time, a great deal more interesting.

2. You learn that what is in your head can't automatically be understood by other people. You realise that you will have to articulate your intentions and feelings with the use of words, and can't blame others for not getting what you mean until you've spoken calmly and clearly.

3. You learn that you do sometimes get things wrong. With courage, you take your first faltering steps towards apologising (once in a while).

4. You learn to be confident not by realising that you're great, but by learning that everyone else is just as stupid, scared and lost as you are. We're all making it up as we go along, and that's fine.

5. You forgive your parents because you realise that they didn't put you on this planet in order to insult you. They were just painfully out of their depth and struggling with demons of their own. Anger turns, at points, to pity and compassion.

6. You learn the enormous influence of so-called 'small' things on mood: bedtimes, blood sugar and alcohol levels, degrees of background stress. As a result, you learn never to bring up an important, contentious issue with a loved one until everyone is well rested, no one is drunk, you've had some food, nothing else is alarming you and you aren't rushing to catch a train.

7. You give up sulking. If someone hurts you, you don't store up the hatred and the hurt for days. You remember you'll be dead soon. You don't expect others to know what's wrong. You tell them straight and if they get it, you forgive them. If they don't, you forgive them in a different way too.

8. You cease to believe in perfection in pretty much every area. There aren't any perfect people, perfect jobs or perfect lives. Instead, you pivot towards an appreciation of what is (to use the psychoanalyst Donald Winnicott's exemplary phrase) 'good enough'. You realise that many things in your life are at once quite frustrating and yet, in many ways, eminently good enough.

9. You learn the virtues of being a little more pessimistic about how things will turn out and, as a result, emerge as a calmer, more patient and more forgiving soul. You lose some of your idealism and become a far less maddening person – less impatient, less rigid, less angry.

10. You learn to see that everyone's weaknesses of character are linked to counterbalancing strengths. Rather than isolating their weaknesses, you look at the whole picture. Yes, someone is pedantic, but they're also beautifully precise and a rock in times of turmoil. Yes, someone is a bit messy, but at the same time brilliantly creative and visionary. You realise that perfect people don't exist and that every strength will be tagged with a weakness.

11. You fall in love a bit less easily. When you were less mature, you could develop a crush in an instant. Now, you're poignantly aware that everyone, however

externally charming or accomplished, would be a bit of a pain from close up. You develop loyalty to what you already have.

12. You learn that you are quite difficult to live with. You shed some of your earlier sentimentality towards yourself. You go into friendships and relationships offering others kindly warnings of how and when you might prove a challenge.

13. You learn to forgive yourself for your errors and foolishness. You realise the unfruitful self-absorption involved in simply flogging yourself for past misdeeds. You become more of a friend to yourself. Of course you're an idiot, but you're still a loveable one, as we all are.

14. You learn that part of what maturity involves is making peace with the stubbornly childlike bits of you that will always remain. You cease trying to be a grown-up at every occasion. You accept that we all have our regressive moments, and when the inner two-year-old you rears its head, you greet them generously and give them the attention they need.

15. You cease to put too much hope in grand plans for the kind of happiness you expect can last for years. You

celebrate the little things that go well. You realise that satisfaction comes in increments of minutes. You're delighted if one day passes by without too much bother. You take a greater interest in flowers and in the evening sky. You develop a taste for small pleasures.

16. What people in general think of you ceases to be such a concern. You realise the minds of others are muddled places and you don't try so hard to polish your image in everyone else's eyes. What counts is that you and one or two others are OK with you being you. You give up on fame and start to rely on love.

17. You get better at hearing feedback. Rather than assuming that anyone who criticises you is either trying to humiliate you or is making a mistake, you accept that maybe it would be an idea to take a few things on board. You start to see that you can listen to criticism and survive it, without having to put on your armour and deny that there was ever a problem.

18. You realise the extent to which you tend to live, day by day, in too great a proximity to certain of your problems and issues. You remember that you need to get perspective on things that pain you. You take more walks in nature; you might get a pet (they don't fret like we do);

and you appreciate the distant galaxies above us in the night sky.

19. You recognise how your distinctive past colours your response to events, and learn to compensate for the distortions that result. You accept that, because of how your childhood went, you have a predisposition to exaggerate in certain areas. You become suspicious of your own first impulses around particular topics. You realise – sometimes – not to go with your feelings.

20. When you start a friendship, you realise that other people don't principally want to know your good news so much as gain an insight into what troubles and worries you, so that they can in turn feel less lonely with the pains of their own hearts. You become a better friend because you see that what friendship is really about is sharing vulnerability.

Taking it a day at a time

Perhaps without us noticing, much of what we place our hopes in will be ready for us in a very long time indeed; in months or even decades from now (if ever): the successful completion of a novel; a sufficient sum of money to buy a house or begin a new career; the discovery of a suitable partner; a move to another country. In the list of our most intensely felt hopes, few entries stand to come to fruition this season or next, let alone by tonight.

But occasionally, life places us in a situation where our normal, long-range, hopeful way of thinking grows impossible. You've been in a car accident; a very bad one. For weeks, it seemed as if you might not make it. You've come out of a coma and are back home, but you still have multiple broken bones, serious bruises and constant migraines. It is unclear when you'll be going back to work, or whether you ever will. When someone asks how things are, one answer seem to fit above all: *we're taking it one day at a time.*

Or imagine that a person is eighty-nine, mentally agile but very slow on their feet and often in pain. They had a fall last month and their left knee is arthritic. Yesterday they did some gardening. Today they may go to the shops for the first time in a while. You ask their carer how they are: *we're taking it one day at a time*.

Or you're a new parent. It was a very difficult birth; the baby had jaundice and required a blood transfusion, but now, finally, mother and child are home. The baby cries a lot in the night and has to take some medicines that aggravate the stomach, but last night was good enough, and hopefully today, if the weather holds, there's a chance of taking a trip to the park to see the daffodils. How is it all going? *We're taking it one day at a time*.

These may be extreme scenarios, and a natural impulse is to hope that we will never encounter them, but they contain valuable teachings for anyone with a tendency to ignore their own advantages; that is, for all of us. One-day-at-a-time thinking reminds us that, in many cases, our greatest enemy is that otherwise critical nectar, hope, and the perplexing emotion it tends to bring with it, impatience. By limiting our horizons to tonight, we are girding ourselves for the long haul and remembering that an improvement may best be achieved when we manage not to await it too ardently. Our most productive mood may be a quiet melancholy, with which we can ward off the temptations of rage or mania and fully imbibe the moderate steadfastness required to do fiddly things: write a book, bring up a child, repair a marriage or work through a mental breakdown.

Taking it day by day means reducing the degree of control we expect to be able to bring to bear on the uncertain future. It means recognising that we have no serious capacity to exercise our will on a span of years and should not therefore disdain a chance to secure one or two minor wins in the hours ahead of us. From a new perspective, we should count ourselves immensely grateful if, by nightfall, there have been no further arguments and no more seizures; if the rain has let off and we have found one or two interesting pages to read.

As life as a whole grows more complicated, we can remember to unclench and smile a little along the way, rather than jealously husbanding our reserves of joy for a finale somewhere in the nebulous distance. Given the scale of what we are up against, knowing that perfection may never occur, and that far worse may be coming our way, we can stoop to accept with fresh gratitude a few of the minor gifts that are already within our grasp.

We might look with fresh energy at a cloud, a duck, a butterfly or a flower. Aged twenty-two, we might scoff at such a suggestion, for there seem so many larger, grander things to hope for than these evanescent manifestations of nature: romantic love, career fulfilment or political change. But with time, almost all one's more revolutionary aspirations tend to take a hit, perhaps a very large one. One encounters some of the intractable problems of intimate relationships. One suffers the gap between one's professional hopes and the available realities. One has a chance to observe how slowly and fitfully the world ever alters in a positive direction. One is fully inducted into the extent of human wickedness and folly – and into one's own eccentricity, selfishness and madness. And so natural beauty may take on a different hue. It is no longer a petty distraction from a mighty destiny, no longer an insult to ambition, but a genuine pleasure amid a litany of troubles; an invitation to bracket anxieties and keep self-criticism at bay; a small resting place for hope in a sea of disappointment; a proper consolation for which one is finally ready, on an afternoon walk, to be appropriately grateful.

Vincent van Gogh (1853–1890) was admitted to the Saint-Paul mental asylum in Saint-Remy in southern France in May 1889, having lost his mind and tried to sever his ear. At the start of his stay, he mostly lay in bed in the dark. After a few months, he grew a little stronger and was able to go out into the garden. It was here that he noticed, in a legendary act of concentrated aesthetic absorption, the gnarled roots of a southern pine, the blossom on an apple tree, a caterpillar on its way across a leaf and – most famously – the bloom of a succession of purple irises. In his hands these became like the totemic symbols of a new religion oriented towards a celebration of the transcendent beauty of the everyday.

Vincent van Gogh, *Irises*, 1890

His painting *Irises* is no sentimental study of a common flower: it is the work of a pivotal figure in Western culture struggling to make it to the end of the day without doing himself in, and clinging on, very tightly indeed, with the hands of a genius, to a reason to live.

It's normal enough to hold out for all that we want. Why would we celebrate hobbling, when we wish to run? Why accept friendship, when we crave passion? But if we reach the end of the day and no one has died, no further limbs have been broken, a few lines have been written and one or two encouraging and pleasant things have been said, then that is already an achievement worthy of a place at the altar of sanity. How natural and tempting to put one's faith in the bountifulness of the years, but how much wiser it might be to bring all one's faculties of appreciation and love to bear on that most modest and easily dismissed of increments: the day already in hand.

Permissions

P. 27 Masaccio, *The Expulsion from the Garden of Eden*, c. 1425. Fresco, 208 cm × 88 cm. Brancacci Chapel, Santa Maria del Carmine, Italy.

P. 40 John Lennon and his son Julian Lennon, c. 1960. Keystone-France / Gamma-Rapho / Getty Images.

P. 51 'since feeling is first'. Copyright 1926, 1954, © 1991 by the Trustees for the E. E. Cummings Trust. Copyright © 1985 by George James Firmage, from COMPLETE POEMS: 1904–1962 by E. E. Cummings, edited by George J. Firmage. Used by permission of Liveright Publishing Corporation.

P. 68 Édouard Manet, *A Bunch of Asparagus*, 1880. Oil on canvas, 46 cm × 55 cm. Wallraf-Richartz-Museum, Cologne, Germany. Darling Archive / Alamy Stock Photo.

P. 77 Philippe de Champaigne, *Still-Life with a Skull vanitas*, c. 1671. Oil on panel, 28 cm × 37 cm. Musée de Tessé, Le Mans, France.

P. 129 Johannes Vermeer, *The Little Street*, c. 1657–1658. Oil on canvas 54.3 × 44 cm. Rijksmuseum, Amsterdam, Netherlands. Accession number: SK-A-2860.

P. 130 Thomas Jones, *A Wall in Naples*, c. 1782. Oil on paper laid on canvas, 11.4 cm × 16 cm. The National Gallery, London, England.

P. 141 Pablo Picasso, *Academic Study*, 1895. Charcoal and black pencil strokes on laid paper, 47 cm × 61 cm. Museu Picasso, Barcelona, Spain. Gift of Pablo Picasso, 1970, MPB 110886. Photo: Gasull Fotografia © Succession Pablo Picasso, VEGAP, Madrid 2020.

P. 141 Pablo Picasso, *The Pigeons*, 1957. Oil on canvas, 100 cm × 80 cm. Museu Picasso Museum, Barcelona, Catalonia, Spain. agefotostock / Alamy Stock Photo.

P. 148 Alberto Giacometti, *View on the Sils Lake Towards Piz Lizun*, 1920. Watercolour on paper, 22 cm x 28 cm. © Alberto Giacometti Estate / Licensed in the UK by ACS and DACS, 2020.

P. 149 Alberto Giacometti, *Ottilia*, c. 1920.
Oil on cardboard, 42.1 cm × 27 cm.
© Alberto Giacometti Estate / Licensed in the UK by ACS and DACS, 2020.

P. 150 Alberto Giacometti, *Walking Man I*, 1960.
Bronze cast, 180.5 cm × 27 cm × 97 cm.
© The Estate of Alberto Giacometti (Fondation Giacometti, Paris and ADAGP, Paris), licensed in the UK by ACS and DACS, London 2020 / Bridgeman Images.

P. 152 Le Corbusier, Villa Savoye, 1928–1931. © F.L.C. / ADAGP, Paris and DACS, London 2020.

P. 159 Francis Bacon, *Turning Figure*, 1962.
Oil on canvas 198 cm x 145 cm. Private collection.
Photo: Prudence Cuming Associates Ltd © The Estate of Francis Bacon. All rights reserved, DACS/Artimage 2020.

P. 177 Paul Cézanne, *Apples*, c. 1878–1879.
Oil on canvas, 22.9 cm × 33 cm. Metropolitan Museum of Art, New York, USA. Accession number: 61.103.

P. 177 Albrecht Dürer. *The Great Piece of Turf*, 1503.
Watercolour, pen and ink, 40.3 cm × 31.1 cm. Albertina Museum, Vienna, Austria. Accession number: W.346.

P. 196 Vincent van Gogh, *Irises*, 1890.
Oil on canvas, 92.7 cm × 73.9 cm. Van Gogh Museum,
Amsterdam, Netherlands, Vincent van Gogh Foundation.

The School of Life is a global organisation helping people lead more fulfilled lives. It is a resource for helping us understand ourselves, for improving our relationships, our careers and our social lives – as well as for helping us find calm and get more out of our leisure hours. We do this through films, workshops, books, gifts and community. You can find us online, in stores and in welcoming spaces around the globe.

theschooloflife.com